ASTROLOGICAL

LANGUAGE

Tito Maciá

Astrological Language

Tito Maciá

Index

Introduction to

Astrological Language

To study any science, it is necessary first to know the language in which it is expressed since how different cultural modalities express themselves is not always through words or concrete concepts.

In "formal" sciences, such as mathematics, chemistry, or physics, mathematical abstractions, geometric abstractions, and concrete language are used to express the astrological cultural phenomenon, we use mathematical abstractions and geometric angles united to symbolic language.

In both cases, these are languages inherited from the cultural traditions of the peoples that have preceded us in time whether we are talking about mathematics or astrology.

To a certain extent, astrology can be compared to pure mathematics, both are very old and related sciences, so much so that in the beginning they were united, even today, the way to designate a mathematician and an astrologer in India is done through the same word.

This language that we astrologers use is in no way irrational, it only has a different logical development order, as is the case with other cultural manifestations such as music, the arts, or psychoanalysis.

The mechanism of the human mind is not a computer program subject to a single code of communication, perception, or understanding of the reality that surrounds us. We do not only think using words or numbers, but we also think in images.

Our way of thinking is not different from that of primitive man, except that modern man has developed different languages with different signs to express words or thoughts.

The primitive man, upon returning to the cave after a difficult hunting day, could only narrate what had happened through sounds accompanied by gestures and images, as can still be seen in certain outcrops of cave paintings. The repetition of these images reduced them to symbols until they formed words and finally a language.

The language of astrology is a compound of symbols and archetypes or patterns of human behavior. This language is very similar to the process of synthesizing thought, once learned it is akin to any other language the astrological language transcends natural linguistic borders and is universal.

It does not matter the nationality, race, sex, or the original language of each person. Understanding astrological language is more similar to understanding music, the arts, or the human soul, than to the numerical count of mathematics or the endless classification of botanical species.

The symbolic language and the understanding of archetypes are learned by activating the right side of the brain, near the area of the musical sense, the sense of humor, and the religious sense, that is, the side of the abstract mind.

Humans in the past – who originated the culture in which we are currently living – reasoned with numbers and geometric figures to solve problems of all kinds, both in the practical realm and in the realm of abstract concepts. These same geometric and numerical reasonings were also applied to solve human and religious problems.

The astrology of our time has remained between these two realms and is applied preferably to solve human problems, maintaining a numerical and geometric language, and another related to archetypes or primordial models that retain the names of the ancient gods, in such a way that in astrology it is very common to talk about gods, geometric figures, and numbers.

In astrological language, numbers, geometric angles, and gods are understood differently than they are by applied sciences when they use numbers and geometry, and of course, the reference to gods has nothing to do with current religious concepts.

In astrological language, we use the names of the ancient gods in a symbolic sense, not religious or mystical. For us, the ancient gods are like morphogenetic fields of memory that act as patterns of behavior that are embedded in the collective unconscious of humanity, that affect us in a significant way, and that are possible to know.

From an astrological point of view, archetypes are pure human models, patterns of behavior that unite us with the sky, and allow us to know ourselves better, but they have nothing to do with religious or mystical sentiment.

The gods we talk about in Astrology can only be the veiled and split reflection of an inextricable mystical presence, intimate with itself.

The path that the astrologer walks along borders the illuminated path along which the truth runs, that is, the experience of the "Being".

However, Astrology cannot be considered a "path" or "way" of realization, at most, a difficult and not recommended path, as there are few mystical astrologers.

So when we talk about gods, we never refer to the "Being", we only refer to the split veils that we perceive.

In such a way that the gods of Astrology are only the shadow on a veil, of truth even greater that transcends the student of this science. Therefore, in astrological interpretation, the words "gods" or their particular names are empty of religious or mystical content, on the other hand, they are full of symbolism and archetypes or human behavioral patterns as we will see later.

To understand astrological language, it is necessary to have prior knowledge of the myths and legends that give meaning and life to these models or human behavioral patterns.

It is undeniable that the greatest concern of the human being, or what has mattered most to him at all times, has been the knowledge of himself. That is why, before the existence of written language and from very ancient times, the ways of being or behaving that are recurrent in human beings or that have left sufficiently notable traces for their registration to be of interest have been collected.

During at least 50,000 years of interglacial life, with a climate similar to that of present-day Brazil and as a nomadic species, neither the size of the human brain nor its intelligence has varied much in these years, but the information we have about ourselves and our environment has changed, thanks to the ability to transmit information from one generation to another – not because there is a brain difference between those who inhabited the planet

30,000 years ago – and us current humans. – This is how important communication transmission is.

Before the existence of written language, our ancestors designed images in the sky that are a treasure trove of symbolic content and archetypes, patterns of behavior that have been recorded in the sky. The myths and legends, which have their stories written in images composed of the constellations and the planets, play the role of mnemonic rules that have allowed us to retain a large amount of information.

In astrological language, each celestial body has a god's name, each constellation has a legend, a myth, and a symbolism loaded with concepts that are fundamentally human patterns of behavior that have been written in the firmament. Each of these myths or legends is like hermetic boxes, which when opened show us rich expressive content, a faithful reflection of a parcel of the collective unconscious of humanity.

The starry sky and the movement of the planets are like a huge cinema screen full of messages written in symbolic language, messages that contain precious information that speaks about the human being, about ourselves, and allows us to know the reason for the behavior of certain human groups, at the same time that they are the bond that unites us with the sky, the divine ray that illuminates our consciousness. But this is a message that comes written in symbols and not in words.

The fundamental characteristic, the best and extraordinary thing about the symbolism and archetypes that we use in Astrology, is its multiplying nature. Because while they represent a certain planetary force or a sector of the sky, they mean a type of human expression, a mode of behavior recurrent in human behavior.

Psychologists, to a certain extent, operate in the same way. They designate a pathological behavior as the Oedipus complex, based on the same mythological sources as we do in Astrology, the difference is that in Psychology they operate with patterns of behavior considered pathological, while astrologers operate with models of behavior that are not pathological, and that contain and allow us to recognize all human patterns of behavior.

Every astrological symbol or archetype identifies a type of person, thing, place, or event, and allows us to reveal the effects that can be expected from astrological influence in the personal or individual sphere.

Jung, one of the great psychologists and thinkers of the last century who dared to include Astrology in the field of his research on human behavior, said: *"The symbol is a language of images and emotions based on expressive and precise condensation that speaks of transcendent truths, external to the human being, −cosmic order −and of inner feelings− thought, moral order, soul evolution−"*

That cosmic order is symbolically written in the sky, and to understand a little of that symbolic language we can think of a gigantic microchip capable of storing and recycling accurate and concise information. The symbolic language that we use in Astrology is a whole psycho-machinery capable of transforming energy and expressing precise concepts.

Another of the great psychologists who have left their mark on the thought of the last century is Cirlot, who affirms that: *"The symbol is an almost exclusively psychic reality that is projected onto nature, either taking its beings as idiomatic elements* (as it happens in astrological symbolism when we use the forms of certain animals) *or by transforming them into characters that participate in the drama of each individual."*

The entire framework that contains the most information about the dramas that each of us can live is reflected or previously written in the legends and myths of the mythological characters who develop to perfection all the ways of behaving in analogous situations of life and that at the same time that they are written in the sky, they are a faithful reflection of our unconscious world.

The symbol cannot be known by itself, because in the symbol the particular represents the general, not as in a dream or a shadow, but as a living and momentary revelation of the inscrutable. As Saurier says: *They are the synthetic expression of a wonderful science of which human beings have lost the memory — but that — teach all that has been and will be, in an unperturbed form.*

Astrological symbolism and its archetypes are part of a language that transcends the physical, linguistic, and temporal barriers of all human beings. It is an immutable language, but it is possible to learn it, and it is one of the most important keys to self-knowledge.

A large part of the work of the astrologer and the psychologist consists of remembering, clarifying, updating, and bringing to individual consciousness the message contained in the symbols and archetypes to help us know what are the patterns of behavior that govern our consciousness.

To facilitate the task of learning astrological symbolism, I will develop a whole series of behavioral models related to these celestial models that correspond, for the most part, to the classical gods, taking care to take the function of that symbolism or behavioral patterns as a pedagogical element.

Finally, it is worth remembering that to understand and use correspondences and analogies, it is convenient to use the artistic sense because as Coommaraswany, an orientalist scholar, and specialist in Indian, Persian, and Arabic art, says: "Symbolism is the art of thinking in images."

The image of Pallas Athena born from the head of her father Jupiter, or the image of Venus Aphrodite born from the foam of the sea, not only have an aesthetic content but represent a different mode of expression of the feminine nature that affects all women. Just like the rest of the astrological models, they act or manifest themselves openly on different

types of people.

The Language of Symbols

The language of symbols is abstract and surreal, but the language of astrological symbolism has a structure, as ordered and organized as any other type of language, a form of expression that must be exercised to be understandable. The first and simplest symbolic graphism that can be represented is a point (.).

Let us reflect for a moment, leaving aside the sense of logic, let us observe from an abstract, artistic, symbolic point of view.

To proceed with the reading of the point, which is the first symbol to be understood, we have to make a mental effort to enlarge it in size until we construct a circle.

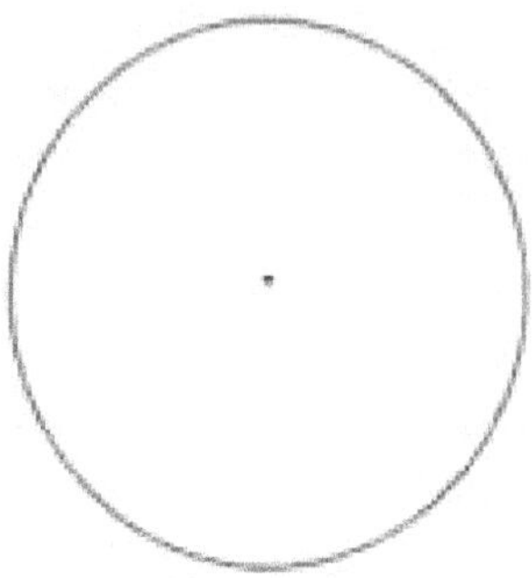

The circle with the point in the center is the symbolic representative of unity, the most important of all symbols because everything is contained in the point. A little strong abstraction, I know, but it is convenient to learn to perceive the largest in the smallest, this is how the symbolic universe is, nothing to do with logic.

Unity is the most abstract, unknown, and difficult to understand the symbol. The only way to approach the understanding of its meaning is through duality. One of the first axioms in symbolism states that:

"All manifestation is dual in principle."

In the case of the point or the circle, we can imagine it as an object whose external form seeks to manifest itself, an object that shows its external part that is perfectly visible, but an object that at the same time contains an internal part that hides an unknown, unknown, and internal meaning.

A clear example of this is when we stand in front of an astrological chart, which we know as an astrological mandala. -We will be able to observe known symbols, we will recognize those symbols of planets, signs, and aspects, but the meaning or interpretation of those symbols remains hidden or internal. -

From here, the first differentiated schemes arise: "the masculine" - represented by what we can see, such as numbers, signs, aspects, etc. - and the "feminine", which corresponds to the hidden part, what we cannot see in principle, the inner meaning of the astrological mandala, which is then interpreted.

In astrological symbolism, the masculine represents the active principle, the first generating impulse, the positive, assimilated to light and heat;

and the feminine, on the contrary, is the passive support, the fertile, the negative, analogous to magnetism, to the cold and dark receptive earth.

To graphically represent the symbol of duality, it is enough to imagine the circle we have described as a sphere, and mentally proceed to turn it 90º.

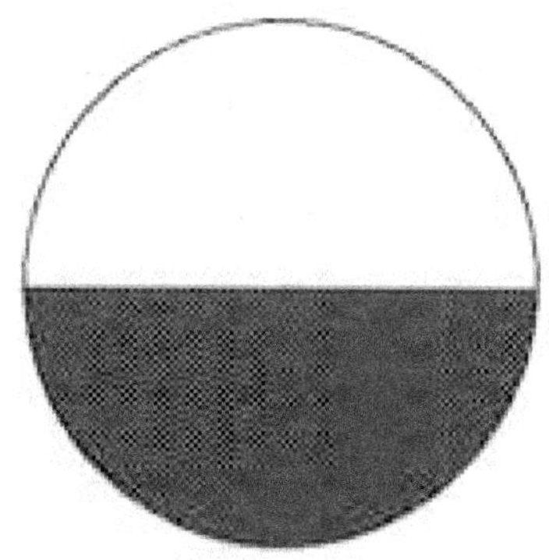

Then what is behind would partially appear, that is, the feminine aspect, what could not be seen, remaining as graph no. 2.

But the true universal symbol of the graphical manifestation of the unity in complete and dual form appears when mentally pushing the masculine force in a direction of rotation as if it had its impulse; that push will produce a reflux of the passive feminine within the masculine.

In the area gained by the masculine, there will always be something feminine and vice versa; in such a way that we would return to the ancestral sign of Ying-Yang.

From this duality of positive-negative, light-magnetism, action-reception, and heat-cold, a new element is born that comes to form the "triplication".

At the moment, when this third element appears, the two previous ones change in appearance and name.

In the "triplication", the masculine principle is transformed into "cardinal", the feminine becomes "fixed" and the third element is established as "mutable".

The cardinal maintains potentialities of masculine-active and assumes traits of movement, impulse, of propulsive force that impels, acts, and moves.

The fixed retains feminine qualities and acquires gradations of stability, firmness, and concentration.

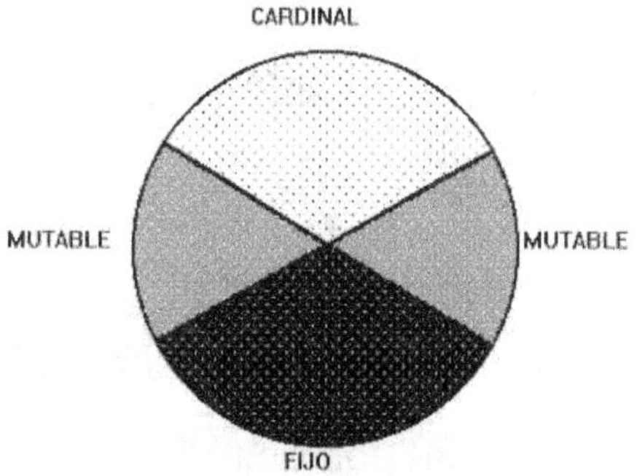

Mutable is dual, and it has masculine and feminine qualities at the same time, acquiring characteristics of variability and change. (Fig. 4) From the third unstable element, and the absorption of the first two, a fourth element appears that will form the "quadruplicity": FIRE, EARTH, AIR, and WATER.

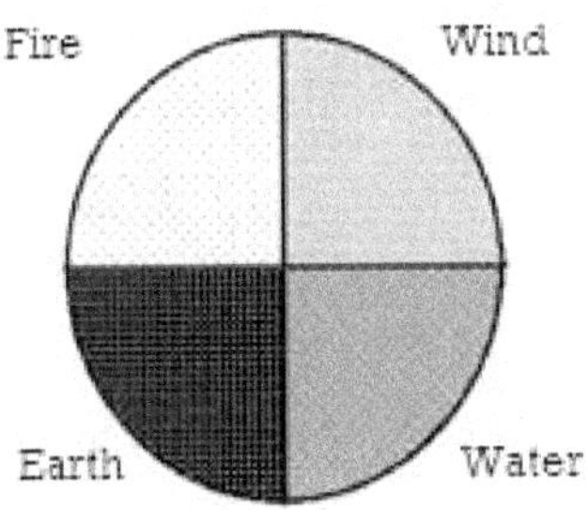

Fire maintains the qualities of the masculine and cardinal, acquiring aspects of pure energy, clarity, dilation, excess heat, and active and luminous movement.

Earth retains feminine and fixed qualities, to which it adds solidity and morphogenesis, representing the object, the concrete, the receptacle, and the fertile.

Air acquires masculine, cardinal, and mutable qualities, gaining aspects of communication and adaptation.

Water retains feminine, fixed, and mutable qualities, transforming the object into plasticity, sensitivity, and calm.

The areas that delimit each of the elements correspond to the primitive qualities of the elements, which are also four: HOT, DRY, COLD, and HUMID.

Between Fire and Earth appears DRY; between Earth and Water, is COLD; between Water and Air is HUMID, and between Air and Fire appears HOT.

Zodiac Signs and Elements

The zodiac signs form different groups based on the affinities of the elements that compose them. The first classification divides the signs into Masculine and Feminine.

-This is the same as saying that there are exteriorizing and interiorizing celestial zones, or centrifugal and centripetal zones.

In any case, in symbolism, when we talk about a masculine or feminine element, we are talking about absolutely abstract elemental principles that have nothing to do with sexuality.

<u>Polarities</u>

Polarities are the first division of the signs so there are masculine signs and feminine signs.

The MASCULINE signs are the following:

Aries, Gemini, Leo, Libra, Sagittarius, Aquarius

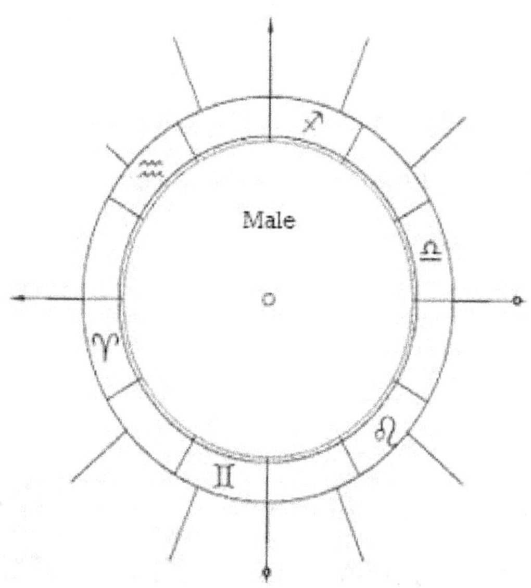

The FEMININE signs are:

Taurus, Cancer, Virgo, Scorpio, Capricorn, Pisces

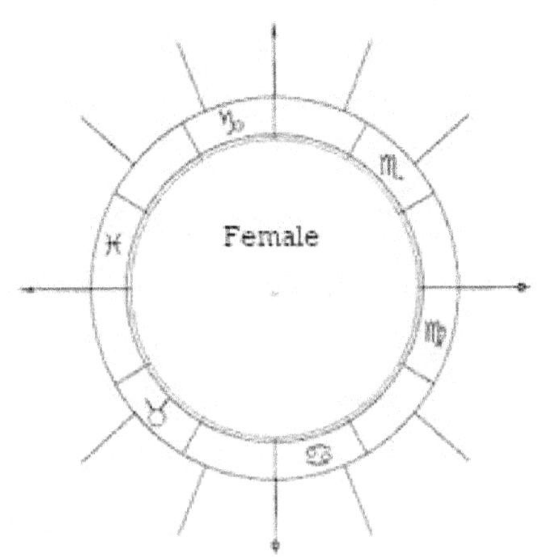

Impulses

The next way to classify and divide the zodiac signs is based on the triplicities, which can be: CARDINAL FIXED or MUTABLE.

The CARDINAL signs are:

Aries, Cancer, Libra, Capricorn

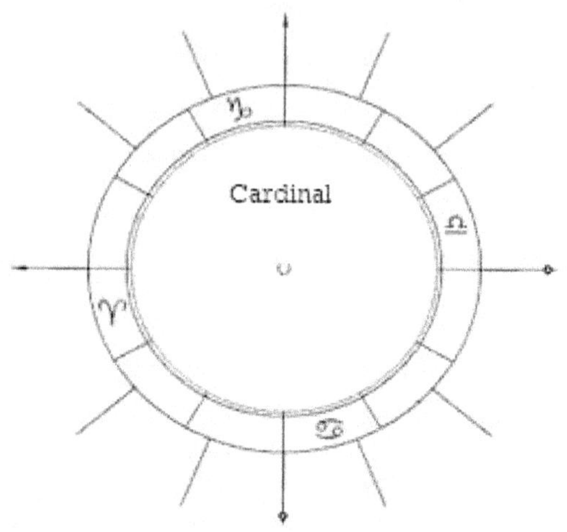

The FIXED signs are:

Taurus, Leo, Scorpio, Aquarius

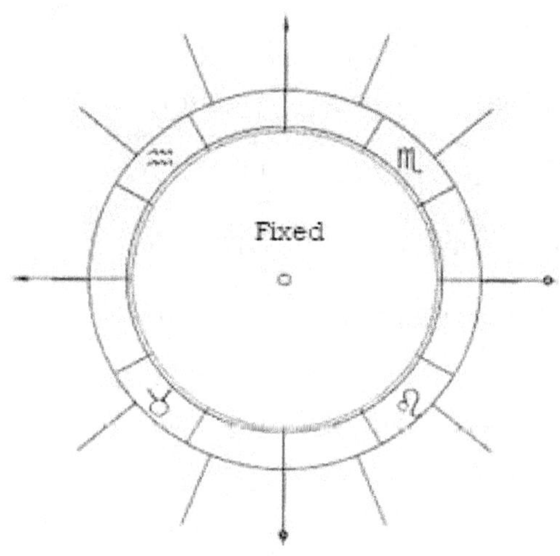

The MUTABLE signs are:

Gemini, Virgo, Sagittarius, Pisces

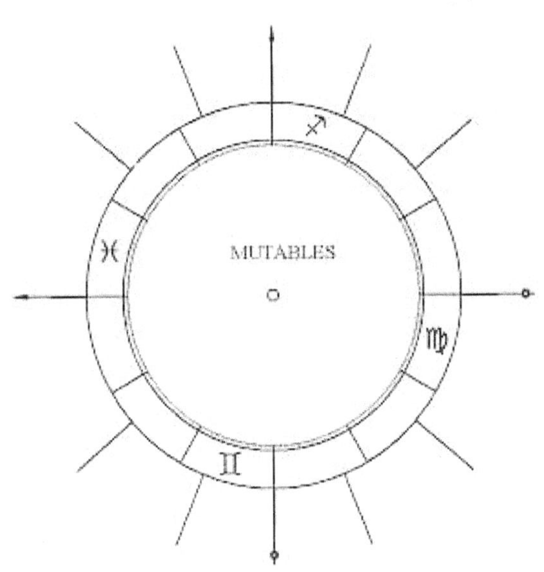

Elements

The third way to classify by affinities is established by the elements, which are four: FIRE, EARTH, AIR, and WATER

The signs of FIRE are: ARIES, LEO, and SAGITTARIUS

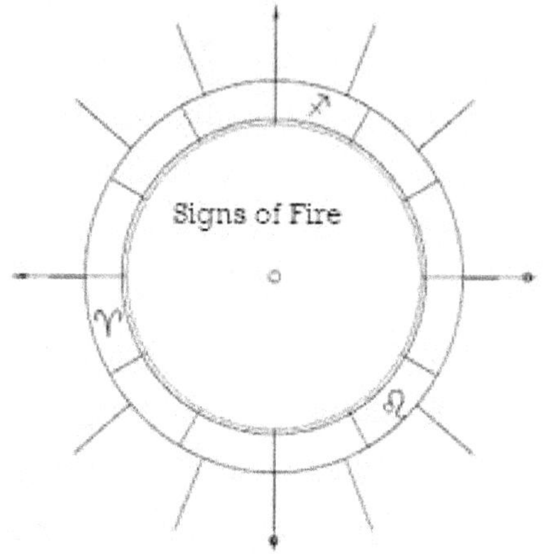

The signs of EARTH are: TAURUS, VIRGO, and CAPRICORN

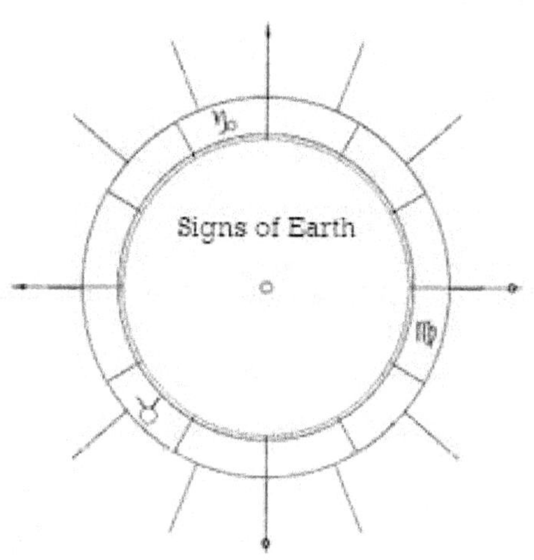

The signs of AIR: GEMINI, LIBRA, and AQUARIUS

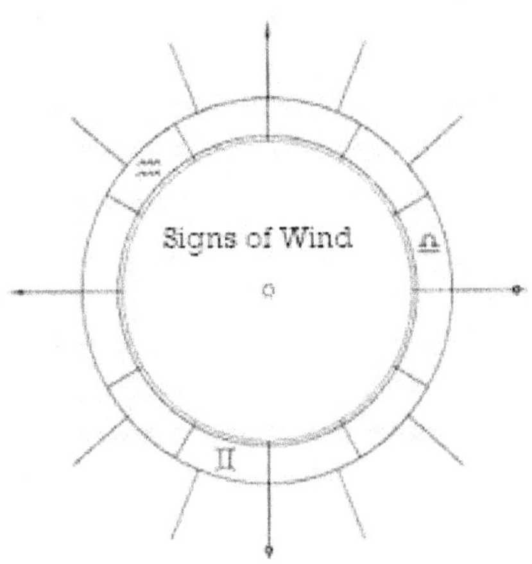

The signs of WATER: CANCER, SCORPIO, and PISCES

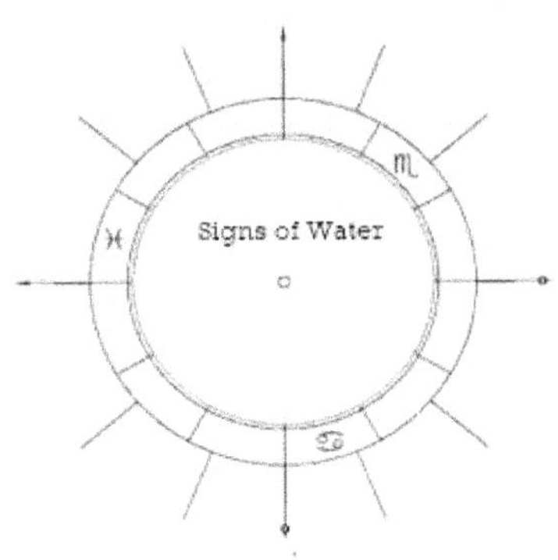

Allegorical Development of
the Four Elements

FIRE

The symbolism of Fire and the rest of the elements is very broad and abstract. First, it symbolizes the active creative force, the engine of periodic regeneration. However, here we will only develop the most elementary allegories that correspond to the astrological signs and we will not delve into any deeper symbolism.

The three signs of Fire provide us with three different nuances of the same symbolic concept.

The first fire, the fire of Aries, represents the spark that ignites everything. It is the incipient fire and it is associated with the smallest but most active particle of fire. The fire of Aries is a flash or a spark that activates the initial flash. In an esoteric sense, the fire of Aries is the initiatory fire.

The second fire, that of Leo, is associated with the fire of the home, of the kitchen stove. The fire of Leo is the constant flame that warms just like the suffocating heat of August. It represents the purifying and regenerating fire. With the fire of Leo, all cooking is done, it is the fire of creation.

The fire of Sagittarius is associated with embers, coals, and the remains of bonfires that burn without flame, it is the fire of stoves, the pleasant heat that allows approach. In another sense, it is the spiritual fire, the desire to ascend like fire or fall towards the sky.

EARTH

Earth is a symbol of consistency and solidity, of concrete and palpable issues. Making allegories with the different nuances of the Earth element, we can imagine the earth of Taurus as the fertile land of valleys and orchards, the irrigated fields where delicious vegetables are produced.

The earth of Taurus is always green and fresh, it represents lush spaces, fruit valleys, and paradisiacal places.

The earth of Virgo is analogous to the land of dry fields where cereals are produced. Virgo is also associated with desert or semi-desert areas where plants develop thorns and spikes such as cacti or prickly pears. The earth of Virgo is always dry or already harvested land.

In Capricorn, the Earth element takes a very different nuance, here it is associated with high lands where rocks appear, they are mountainous or rocky lands. They are places suitable for the development of goat livestock.

AIR

The symbolism of air is linked to the world of ideas, thought, exchange, and mobility. It represents breath and participation. The air signs can also be nuanced by using the allegories of the winds.

The air of Gemini can be associated with the fresh breezes of early summer and the cool breezes from the sea. The air of Gemini is analogous to the lively and pleasant winds that come to clear the atmosphere.

The air of Libra is associated with hot winds, the warm and sensual air of late summer. This air is analogous to the terrestrial winds that are always warm but sometimes uncomfortable. They are the winds that can eventually bring autumn storms.

The air of Aquarius is associated with the winds of February, with the gales, the cold and harsh winds that stir everything up. It is the cold air that drags with it the motionless and harsh winter. It is the air that seeps through the cracks and always feels cold and penetrating.

WATER

The symbolism of water encompasses the entire world of feelings and emotions. It is sex in the purest and coldest sense, which expands and rises by the effect of fire. The first water sign is Cancer, the crab, so we will associate the water of Cancer with the aquatic places where these crustaceans live. The water of Cancer changes constantly, it is the water of the riverbank and the shores of the seas, it is the water that runs or that changes with its waves, the moving water of beaches and rivers.

The water of Scorpio has a double analogy, it is the extreme water; it can be the incredible and crystal-clear water of caves, the underground water, it is also the water that flows through the orifice of the fountains, and, on the other hand, it is the water of ponds and swamps, the putrid and corrupt water of the ponds.

Finally, the water of Pisces is the boundless water of the seas and oceans. The water of Pisces is the liquid of the almost infinite marine spaces where only water exists without limits. The water of Pisces is also the water that evaporates and forms clouds, it is the celestial water of the clouds that transforms into rain.

Symbolism of the Sun

The Sun is the most evident and important celestial body for us, so in Astrology, it is the most revered symbol since antiquity.

Because it is the most powerful celestial body, it is also the most vivid and objective symbol for human perception.

The Sun is the center of our planetary system, and it is also the center of our symbolic sky. In both cases, it represents the force that makes everything revolve around it.

The Sun is the universal symbol of the king, the heart of the kingdom, and it represents the principle of authority, and nobility of heart, so it is associated, in the human body, with the heart.

The Sun represents the most important celestial body, both in real and symbolic terms.

-Jung says: *"The different aspects of what is endowed with psychic vital force, of the extraordinarily efficient – of the concept of personified mana, come together in the character of Rudra (the flaming Sun of white radiance, the beautiful helmet, the bull of procreative vigor) and urine (from urine = to burn)."*

-Not only the gods but also the goddesses, considered from the point of view of their dynamics, are symbols of libido. The Sun represents the point from which the greatest content of libido emanates. For astrologers, all human beings are like a small cosmos with the sun as the center of their consciousness.

-Libido is expressed in metaphors of sun, light, fire, sexuality, fertility, and growth. This is also why the goddesses have phallic symbols, although these are essentially masculine.

One main reason for this is that just as there is something feminine in men, there is something masculine in women.

-This explanation made by Jung clarifies that, although the Sun is assigned a masculine symbolism, the source of libido, there is no differentiation between man-woman and male-female.

In the field of Astrology, all human beings are considered to be microcosms with a central Sun.

To clarify the topic, Jung says: *"It can be said that in the psychological field, the concept of libido has the same importance as the concept of "energy" in physics since Robert Mayer."*

When we observe a person's birth chart, the Sun tells us about the prospects for the expansion of individual libido, it shows us the original center of the vital impulses of each person.

The Sun in Astrology represents the center of the conscious mind, that is, the strongest psychological function that is associated with the Ego, the Self.

The Sun, like the Ego or like the libido impulses, is not something stable or static.

The Sun emits prominences, jets, or flares that last for several days and reach heights of over a million kilometers; by analogy, the Ego and the libido are also manifested in waves, with variable intensities, often encompassing extra-individual spaces.

Periodically, dark spots appear on the Sun, forming nuclei in which the temperatures drop by more than a thousand degrees and become intensely dark; analogously, dark and cold areas appear in the libido and the Ego that cannot or do not know how to manifest themselves at certain times.

Almost all the light and heat that makes life possible on our planet emanates from the Sun; by analogy, in its astrological approach, it corresponds to the vitality of each individual, with their life force.

The Sun emits mainly in an outward direction, it illuminates and warms its entire system, and for this reason, it represents all the exteriorizations of the Ego.

In another sense, the symbolism of the Sun is directly related to the creative abilities of each person and their creative manifestations. The outward activity of the Sun is comparable to the generous impulses of the ego and to the fiery spirit that provokes enthusiasm and induces life.

Solar energy manifests itself in the growth and development of life; by analogy, from Astrology, it is associated with the prospects for ascent in life and the possibilities for the development of each individual.

In its negative aspect, we can see the Sun as a gigantic magnetic mass that traps the rest of the planets. This negative or feminine aspect of the Sun is well known to Eastern astrologers, who consider it the "great malefic".

These solar gravitational forces are analogous to the selfish desires that all living beings possess. It is the influence that induces excessive and immoderate self-love, which is sometimes disguised by appearing to arise from noble causes or personal merits, but which in general tend to end in vanity or, in the worst cases, in pride.

This dark and magnetic part of the Sun is the closest thing to the blindness of selfishness that leads sooner or later to the collapse of the heart, both in a metaphorical and real sense, where circulation is prevented and life ends. This is the "malefic" aspect of the Sun.

All the planets revolve around the Sun and follow their trajectory in space; by analogy, the individual sphere, is related to personal organizational capacity, will, individual dominance, authority exercised over others, and personal influences in the environment.

The Sun is the most important focus of attention in the consciousness of each person. It is equivalent to self-love, pride, dignity, or personal prestige. From this point, our impulses emerge toward acquisition, the search for reputation, recognition, or fame.

The Sun in the natal chart represents the ambitions of each person and indicates the individual's tendencies to make themselves worthy of special attention. It also shows us their degree of honesty and the scope of their actions.

The Sun, within a natal chart, is undoubtedly the most important focus of attention, the point of greatest personal identification, the most valued and sensitive, that which most determines and conditions the responses of each person to the environment that surrounds them.

The Sun, like the rest of the astrological symbolism, has a reading in depth, towards the interior. It is something like reading in the different layers of an onion; once the reading has been carried out in one layer, or at one level of interpretation, the next is removed and opened, and so on, until the mind of the interpreting astrologer can reach it.

The symbolism of the Sun not only encompasses personal expressions but also shows us how we relate to our surroundings and other people. It symbolizes certain places, objects, and people in the environment of each individual, as well as certain events that surround the life of each person.

The Sun corresponds to and therefore can manifest itself through those characters who possess some type of authority or who represent dignity for each person, such as certain relatives, bosses, patrons, or anyone who exercises some dominance over us. On the other hand, it also represents the most noble, powerful, or influential contacts that can be reached. For a married woman, it represents her husband.

Continuing with the multiplier nature of the symbol, the Sun can be related to bright, warm, and spacious places. In other words, it is in these places where solar symbolism is preferably staged. If we refer to places in general, we can talk about very bright and warm places, the most spacious and bright center of the house, large well-lit living rooms, and all those places where light and spaciousness predominate.

In the home environment, it is related to the living room and the large windows through which the sun enters.

The Sun can also be related to all those objects that have shine or that are valuable. It is also comparable to all golden or luxurious objects.

About foreseeable events, it corresponds to stagings of life with brilliant, honest, truthful results, and that denotes generosity. Its influence is staged through events that grant increases in dignity, such as merits, power, or greatness.

The Sun is active or its influence is staged in moments when personal merits and all those brilliant and worthy individual qualities are manifested.

Although in many cases, only the magnetic aspect of the Sun manifests itself, appearing then in situations in which misunderstood self-love creates the worst deviations of personal destiny, such as when we feel hurt by our pride.

The symbolism of the Sun also has an archetypal content, it contains an ideal prototype, an eternal, immaterial, immutable, and perfect model, a model that the human being tries to imitate, as a fashion is imitated but in a much more intense and subtle way.

The Sun stages its influence on each of us through the attraction that the model to imitate exerts, a "mold of man", in Castaneda's terminology; this archetype is very well explained in myths and legends, with its disparate personifications, according to cultures and times, as we will see later.

Within the astrological structure, the Sun has its Domicile in the zodiac sign of Leo, its Exaltation in Aries, its Detriment in Aquarius, its Fall in Libra, its Joy in the 9th House, and its Sadness in the 3rd House.

Each planet has an age at which its manifestation is easier. The Sun covers the ages between 24 and 43 years. This is a time of self-affirmation in the world, of seeking personal, social, or professional recognition, it is a stage in life of developing organizational capacity where the will has more possibility of governing.

The Pure Solar Model

The solar model is always represented by a hero. In the Piscean model, it is a religious hero, so descending from the pure and primordial models to a more human level, we can imagine the solar model in the form of a hero. This model is inserted in each of us and tends to express itself from the deepest parts of our being.

When this solar archetype is dominant in an individual, it can transform or shape his physical appearance.

When this happens, people appear, men or women, of powerful appearance, well-formed, with long bones, large faces, and forehead, fair skin, short noses, wavy hair, rounded eyes, angular faces tending to hexagonal, wide chest and arms longer than the trunk.

The psychological characteristics of this human model usually manifest themselves through a personality of powerful character, with good organizational skills, high ideals, full of self-confidence, affection, and burning passions, but sensitive to wounds in self-love. – As is the case with people born under the sign of Leo or those who have the Sun or Leo in the ascendant.

Keywords of the Sun

Character, destiny, and trends

Ambitious: With aspirations for success and recognition.

Dignified: With a strong sense of honor and integrity.

Voluntary: With a great capacity for leadership and decision-making.

Establisher: With a drive towards stability and security.

Individualist: With a strong sense of individuality and independence.

Truthful: With a strong sense of honesty and justice.

Organizer: With a great ability to plan and organize.

Magnificent: With a big heart and a willingness to help others.

Objects and Places

Golden objects: Represent wealth, power, and prosperity.

Luxury objects: Represent status, success, and sophistication.

Warm and bright places: Represent energy, vitality, and creativity.

Large windows: Represent openness, clarity, and vision.

Spacious places: Represent freedom, space, and expansion.

Main squares: Represent the center, authority, and power.

Large living rooms: Represent elegance, luxury, and sophistication.

Solar Archetype, the Sun Deity

The representative model of the solar archetype varies depending on the time and culture from which it manifests itself.

For us, of Mediterranean culture, those models inherited from the cultures that have preceded us in time and that are still alive and valid in our collective unconscious are more interesting and understandable.

In all cases, the solar model always represents the brightest archetype of our unconscious. It is, as I said before, the "mold of man" that Carlos Castaneda defines.

To unravel and know the model in its purest form, myths, and legends have been written. Going back to the models of the oldest cultures that have been able to affect us, leaving us an unconscious footprint, we first find the solar model represented by Vishnu, who rules over a golden sky and bears the symbol of the Sun as an emblem.

This original prototype is assigned different names or epithets as characteristics or attributions that define it.

They call him *Svayambhu, the one who exists by himself; Ananta, the infinite; Yajñevara, the lord of sacrifice; Hari, the raptor, the one who takes possession of souls to save them.*

Janarddana, the one who captures the adoration of the people; Makunda, the liberator.

Madhava, the one who has been formed of honey; Keçava,

the one with long hair,

his hair is the sun's rays

and Narayana, the source and refuge of beings.

This solar divinity suffers from torpor equivalent to death or periods of activity and rest. These periods are comparable to the organic rhythm of inspiration-expiration. Each cycle of cultural or religious creation corresponds to an "Avatar", a model by that human cycle.

Avatar means the descent of some god, primordial model, or some glorious being into the body of a simple mortal.

That humanization of the divine or solar model determines the pure and original model that will condition the social behavior of an era and a culture.

Other solar models close to our culture are, on the one hand, the Buddha, (the man of gold, the Sun – Buddha) and on the other hand Apollo who comes out of the Hyperborean world and whose arrow is like a ray of sun.

But for us of Western culture, the second model has probably influenced us much more. The Greek solar model is represented by Apollo – Phoebus, half god, half human.

In his legend, Phoebus (Sun in the sky) also descends to Earth, he is an "avatar" and takes human form under the name of Apollo.

Like all solar models, his first attribution is to be a god of light, a solar deity, which however does not confuse him with this star but makes the model correspond to the epic solar qualities.

Apollo is a solar archetype corresponding to the Age of Aries in Greek civilization. It is linked to Apollo Carneios of the Dorians, that is, the god Ram, an obvious model of the Age of Aries, the Ram.

Like the Piscean model, which we will see below, Apollo never married, although he had numerous relationships and left offspring. Apollo is also a symbol of victory over violence, although at first, he is an irascible warrior, a "master of the beasts", then transforms into a helpful shepherd who protects the flocks.

In this model, the balance and harmony of desires are achieved, not by suppressing human passions, as is the case with Christ, but by orienting them towards a progressive spiritualization, thanks to the development of consciousness.

But the most important solar model for our Western culture is undoubtedly Christ. Jesus appears in our culture as a sun that radiates justice, he is called "Sol iustitiae" and also "Sol Invictus".

The Christogram, a symbolic monogram of Christ, is similar to a solar wheel. For Westerners, and until our time (late 20th century), the model of Christ has been predominant as a solar archetype.

Jesus Christ is undoubtedly the avatar of our Judeo-Christian civilization of the Age of Pisces, recognized as such before he was born by the astrologers who preceded us.

As astrologers, we know that in each Age of each civilization, a solar prototype manifests itself with the nuances of the Age.

The Christ model reflects the solar archetype filtered through the zodiac sign of Pisces, through which the most recently passed Age has passed.

The Piscean message of this model is "total surrender", "dissolution with others", and "we are all one". Here the solar "I" appears to disintegrate with the sublimation of carnal love. With this exemplary baggage, Jesus of Nazareth appears, whose patterns of behavior and moral inclinations will mark and determine the behavior of several billions of people over more than two millennia.

Despite this Piscean nuance, the model retains ancestral characteristics. Like the model represented by Vishnu, Christ is also the *"lord of sacrifice"*, *"the one who takes possession of souls to save them"*, *"the one who captures the adoration of the people"*, *"the liberator"*, and also *"the one with long hair"*.

In the 1960s, more precisely February 1962, the door opens to the beginning of the end of an era. As in any moment of evolutionary crisis, or transformative disturbances, the imitation of the model of the era is irresistible for the nucleus of the most receptive people, that is, the young.

In the 1960s, there was a growing interest in spirituality, new religions, and the use of certain consciousness-expanding substances, such as marijuana, LSD, sacred mushrooms, and entheogenic cacti. This phenomenon, analogous to the symbolism of Neptune, ruler of Pisces, spread through Western culture, causing the amplification of closed individual consciousnesses in the West.

This phenomenon allowed for the inner and personal experience of contact with the archetype. There are thousands of cases of people who experienced the identity of Christ under the effects of certain disciplines or the use of certain drugs. This personal experience unconsciously led to the staging of the primitive model: long, straight hair, long robes, messages of peace and love, etc.

The highest moral values contributed by this solar archetype with Piscean nuances are related to love for others, compassion, etc., expressing the exaltation of Venus in Pisces.

Social behavior patterns have also been conditioned and fixed by this gregarious and unifying model, clearly Neptunian.

"Come after me, and I will make you fishers of men," Jesus said to Peter and Andrew.

On the other hand, the influence of Jupiter, the classical ruler of Pisces, is also felt.

"Do not think that I have come to abolish the law or the prophets, but to fulfill," "...not one iota or one tittle will pass away from the law..." Mt 5:18.

The relationship of this model to imitate, the schemes of Pisces and by correspondence with the twelfth House, also manifests itself.

"Heal the sick, cleanse the lepers..."

This message has allowed for the development of humanitarianism and helping others.

Before the arrival of the Age of Pisces, one of the models to imitate, "the one who captures the adoration of the people," "the one who takes possession of souls to save them," "the liberator," had all the Arian nuances of Ares, Mars for Roman civilization, where it had its greatest splendor and devotion.

Before the model of Christ appeared, there was a warrior and conquering model, necessary for the civilization of that time to develop and expand its culture conveniently.

After this Piscean era, a new model awaits us that, like the previous ones, will capture the adoration of the people and will be the model to imitate. But for the Western world of today, with Christian roots, the figure of Christ is the distant axis – like the Sun – of the moral and social behavior of all of us, so developing all the behavioral patterns that have conditioned this solar model is unnecessary, as we are all, even if we do not realize it, imbued with or under the influence of this well-known model.

Symbolism of the Moon

After the Sun, the Moon is the celestial body that attracts the most attention. It appears behind the Sun, grows, reaches its fullness, then decreases again and disappears behind the rays of the Sun. The Moon is the second most important star on the Earth. Although its size is smaller than that of the other planets, it affects us because of its proximity, it is the star closest to us.

The Sun represents unity and regularity in its cycles, while the Moon symbolizes cyclical irregularity and multiplicity. This disparate and variable characteristic is manifested in the different phases of the Moon, which are symbolically related to the biological rhythms of birth, growth, decline, and death.

After the Sun, the Moon is the star that has the greatest influence on this planet and on the living beings that inhabit it. The luminosity of the Moon produces a significant growth in organic life and its gravitational force is so powerful that it moves the large masses of water in the oceans, causing the tides.

Because it is directly responsible for the movements of the waters, it is associated with liquids, water, and the way we use it, both inside our body and in personal hygiene.

Water, in symbolic language, represents unconscious energies, the unformed powers of the soul, and the secret and unknown motivations that can be associated with "emotions", suggestions, or nostalgia.

The Moon encloses the world in which we live in its orbit, defending the Earth from external impacts; by analogy, it represents the instinct of protection.

Because of its regular variability, it has to do with everything that changes periodically, with the predictable changes in human life.

As a representative of the multiple, it allows us to know the plural, what spreads, and the fertility of each person. This variability is similar to the changes in mood, and the variations in humor, and represents the fickle polarity of the female consciousness.

In its multiple manifestations, it can be seen as white light in the full moon period; as dark absorbing magnetism, when it is new, and as a mixture of both, when it is growing or waning.

The full moon, white and luminous, exerts an influence derived from the sun and is symbolically related to the "white of the east," the white of the dawn, which means the return. The white color of its light, as yellow purified, is the color of intuition and the hereafter, in its affirmative and spiritual aspect.

This lunar white color is also a symbol of purity and hygiene because it expels evil spirits (microbes, viruses, and bacteria), which is why hospitals kitchens, and the places most in need of hygiene are completely white.

The new moon, dark and magnetic, is comparable to the "dull white" of death, to the white of the west that absorbs the being and introduces it into the lunar world, cold and female, which leads to absence, to the nocturnal void, to the disappearance of consciousness and the diurnal colors.

This moon represents, as we will see later with the archetype of Hecate, the jealous, dominating, and castrating aspect of the woman.

In contrast, the full moon represents the active emanation of affections; the affectivity of individuals born with a full moon is directed outward, like lunar light, seeking exteriorization and expansion; for this reason, people born with this type of moon have many more chances of suffering conflicts; in fact, it is an index of lack of affectivity during the first period of life and a risk of repeating this situation at the end.

While the new moon represents a passive affectivity, open to the reception of feelings. Behaving magnetically, it attracts the affections of others. In the waxing or waning moons, there is a balance between the reception and emission of feelings.

The Moon is the mirror of the Sun, the image that each one has of oneself, the point of reference by which one imagines being in a certain way, it is what one identifies with and believes to be.

The Moon, by being the closest or most familiar, stages its influence through the mother, the family, the home, the most immediate every day, and the circle in which we move ordinarily. Like the mother or the family, the Moon represents the past, where we come from, the retrospective, what is recorded in memory, memories, and longings.

The Moon, like the mother, is analogous to milk, food, eating, home, and kitchen....... *"the kitchen, as a place of events, represents the unconscious"* – Jung. The Moon is associated with the unconscious, in contrast to the conscious mind, which was associated with the Sun.

In astrological interpretation, the Moon makes its influence felt through the nature of the instincts, it is the channel of energy from which the faculty of reaction to feelings emanates. Its position within a natal chart will inform us of the way each person feels, of their instinctive way of reacting, and of the mechanism of their emotions.

The human organism is associated with the digestive system, the uterus, the left eye, the breasts, and the adipose tissue.

When the energy of the Moon has not been able to channel well or has not been able to flow, then it condenses in those parts of the body, making us sick.

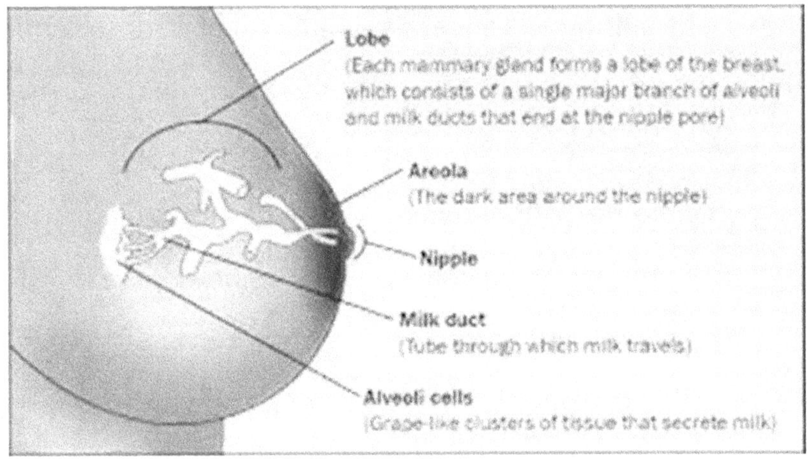

The Moon can also be interpreted about the surrounding world. It can be related to the social environment in which each individual moves.

The Moon is analogous to the people, the most immediate social group. It is the focus of attention that manifests itself in public or social life. For this reason, the Moon is associated with public places, squares, markets, bazaars, souks, etc.

The Moon represents the place of birth, the place where home life originates, where the mother, the woman, or the family is. It is also associated with the feminine world, housewives, mothers, etc.

In another sense, it is also related to cooks, waiters, housing builders, public officials, crowds, masses, etc.

Like the symbolism of the Sun, the Moon also has a content of archetypes or models, that is, it represents human models and patterns of behavior.

Through myths and legends, we will learn about these different female prototypes.

The Moon has its Domicile in the zodiac sign of Cancer, its Exaltation in Taurus, its Detriment in Capricorn, its Fall in Scorpio, its Joy in the 3rd House, and its Sadness in the 9th House.

The age at which the influence of the Moon is perceived most intensely is from 0 to 4 years old.

Keywords of the Moon
Character-Destiny

Imaginative-The   most   common,   the everyday**

Dreamy-The mother, the family, the wife**

Changing-Natural, predictable changes**

Complacent-The instinct of protection**

Traveler-The most immediate social group**

Open-Memories- longings**

Cozy-Food, eating, home**

Maternal-The unconscious, emotions**

Objects and Places -where the lunar influence is openly manifested

Silver objects

The kitchen

Damp places

Public places and squares

Large mirrors (moons)

Interior window

Beaches or banks

Lunar Archetypes. Goddesses of the Moon

Due to the different phases of the Moon, myths and archetypes have had to adjust to these variable aspects. The Moon, as a representative of multiplicity, cannot help but show itself in its multiple faces or facets.

The full moon, round and bright, is assimilated to the mythical model of Artemis of Ephesus, the one with multiple breasts, the great nurturing mother. While Hecate is associated with the representative model of the new and dark moon.

The waxing or waning moon, visible only in the early hours of the night or just before dawn – known as the hours of the hunter – when animals come out of their hiding places and are more active, is the crescent moon and is associated with the model of Artemis or Diana the Huntress, who with her bow in hand, symbolizes the waxing or waning moon.

Roman mythologists very accurately represented this triple lunar character. They erected an image with three faces at the crossroads, thus embodying their triple personality: Artemis in the sky, Diana on earth, and Hecate in the underworld.

The Goddess Artemis

The first lunar model represents the full moon and is associated, among others, with the myth of Artemis of Ephesus, the one with countless breasts, and is astrologically related to the exaltation of the Moon in Taurus. Fittingly, this female deity was also known as the "Tauride".

In ancient legends, Artemis was the goddess of fertility, of vegetative life. Her cult spread throughout the Peloponnese and reached its peak in Asia Minor. The main center of her cult was centered in Ephesus, from where her classical image comes, represented with a kind of crown in the shape of a tower or basket, very similar to the one worn by the Mediterranean goddess Tanit and that belongs to Phoenician mythology, very rooted in the Mediterranean of the eastern coast of Spain. But the most striking thing about this representation is the infinity of nourishing breasts that fill her entire torso.

This exaggeration of breasts is intended to emulate the limitless nourishing capacity of the full moon.

This model is clearly distinguished from that of Artemis -Diana- that will be presented later because far from being a Virgin, she is a true wet nurse.

The universal nurse and protector of all living beings on our planet. In the myth, her fecundating action reached all forms of life, both plant and animal or human. She was considered the protector of the married and the mother of numerous offspring, she was the maternal goddess, the distributor of fertility, and the patroness of childbirth.

The myths about this full moon model are lost in the mists of time, a similar model was already known in Eastern cultures. Then she appeared as the great White Goddess, the great White Sow, as she would later be called. During her festive celebrations in Asia Minor, nursing mothers consecrated their children in the temple of the goddess, and amid dances and a rustic banquet, a little piglet was sacrificed in her honor.

Artemis, as a human prototype, can be associated with the type of woman whose main goal is to find a home and be a mother. She represents the fertile and procreative woman, the originator of the family as a fundamental and essential cell for the preservation of the human species. She is the model of a woman as a mother above all else.

The Diana Model

In classical mythology, Diana is the goddess of the hunt and the forests, and her symbol is a bear.

If we delve into the symbol of the bear, which appears as Diana's companion and whose form she often adopts when she appears, we will obtain a very pure, although unattractive, image of this model imitated by many women. The bear is a symbol of the warrior caste, as opposed to that of the boar, which symbolizes the priestly caste. In Siberia and Alaska, the bear is also assimilated to the Moon, because it disappears cyclically, hiding in winter and reappearing in spring.

She is also associated with the bear because her mysterious breath emanates from the caves. Caves are analogous to the female aspect of the terrestrial orography, clearly opposed to the peaks of the mountains, which are reserved, as we will see later, for priestly symbolism.

In the legend, it is said that she prostrated herself at the feet of her father (Zeus) and, embracing his knees, asked him, instead of jewels or ornaments, a short tunic, a hunter's footwear, a quiver with her arrows, and a bow like the one her brother Apollo had.

For this reason, Diana has the same attributes as Apollo, as he is, she is armed with a bow and quiver, and for this reason, she is called "Apollousa" the destroyer, and also "Iocheaira" the one who takes pleasure in shooting her arrows. Diana is the one who makes unfortunate humans succumb under her fearsome arrows.

Similar to Apollo, Diana is also the goddess of sudden death, and her favorite victims are women.

The legend of Actaeon tells us how this young hunter, one day while chasing prey with his dogs, came to the place near a spring where Diana and her companions were bathing, and amazed by the beauty of the goddess, he lingered too long in observing her and was surprised.

Enraged, Diana, that a mortal had been able to contemplate her nakedness, transformed Actaeon into a stag and delivered him to the greed of his pack.

This aspect of lack of mercy, fierce and destructive is repeated in the legend of Callisto, a virgin hunter-nymph who was part of her retinue, with whom Zeus fell in love.

As in all myths, Zeus would transform himself to approach his lovers. In some legends, it is said that he metamorphosed into the same Artemis to approach the nymph, for Callisto fled from all men to preserve her chastity.

In that disguise, Zeus possessed her. When one day Artemis and her nymphs were bathing, completely naked, at seeing Calisto's undressed body, her pregnancy became evident, as her belly was not as smooth as the others.

Then, Artemis, the cruel guardian of chastity, became enraged, as was her custom whenever something similar happened, and transformed Callisto into a bear and killed her with arrows.

When Zeus learned of the death of his beloved, he was heartbroken. He gathered her spirit and took it to the most important place in the sky, placing it as the most visible constellation in the firmament, the Big Dipper.

Artemis's conscious cruelty also has its unconscious consequences, as is the case in the myth of Orion, with whom Artemis was in love.

One day, while Orion was bathing in the sea and had moved away to the horizon of the coast, Apollo challenged his sister to hit the farthest moving point with an arrow. This point was nothing more than Orion's head, which was playing with the waves in the distance.

Artemis drew her bow, and her arrow pierced her lover's temple. Although other myths say she killed him because he tried to rape her, it seems to be a pattern that repeats itself in a certain class of women who cannot maintain a relationship under normal conditions.

This cruel and destructive attitude of the archetype fits with the woman who is forced to emancipate herself, destroying the man who possessed her and who did not know or could not give her what she demanded. It is the model of a free and fighting woman, lover of freedom, vindicating her rights as an individual equal to man, and represents the prototype of a single, divorced, or celibate woman who applies all her energies to the formation of her world.

In this model, the woman wants to be equal to a man with all his attributes, she does not need luxury, but freedom of action. Something that few men know how to give to their women.

The of the New Moon Hecate

The third lunar model is associated with the new moon or black moon, a period during which the moon does not reflect any light, and is associated with Hecate, the third lunar deity.

This model has similar characteristics to those of Diana, with whom she is sometimes confused. She is erroneously considered a perverse or terrible model because she is the goddess of the souls of the dead. However, as Hesiod affirms, Hecate has a benign and protective aspect. In her legend, she grants men wealth, victory, and wisdom.

In her myths, she appears as the daughter of Zeus and Hera. Many mythologists associate her with Persephone or Proserpina.

It is said that on one occasion she suffered the anger of her mother for stealing her cosmetics to give them to Europa. To avoid maternal punishment, Hecate fled to hide in the house of a woman who had recently given birth. By this contact, she became impure.

Following the story, Hecate, to dispel her impurities, immersed herself in the waters of the Acheron (the river of muddy and bitter waters, the "river of affliction" or the "river of pain"). Through this purification, she became a deity of the underworld, once again associated with Persephone.

In the underworld, she enjoyed great authority. She presided over purifications and expiations, and she protected spells and magical practices. In another legend, it is said that she sent demons to the surface of the Earth, such as the barking of dogs, which are the torment of humans. She got up at night accompanied by her pack of dogs. She never appeared alone but was accompanied by a procession of the souls of those who died a violent death and those who died before their time.

Dogs were the only sacrifice that could be offered to the goddess because it was said that they were the only ones who barked at the moon.

Therefore, the symbolism of the dog is closely linked to the Moon and the zodiac sign of Cancer. A little further south of this constellation, the constellations of the Canes Major and Minor are found, with the bright star Procyon (Head of the dog) and further south, the Can Major, with Sirius, the brightest star in the northern sky, the heart of the Can Major.

In the best representations of the tarot, in the card that corresponds to the Moon, these two dogs also appear. According to the interpretation of Stanislas de Guaita, the dogs bark at the Sun in its annual orbit, to warn it that it has reached the culmination of its trajectory.

However, most of the symbolic meaning of the lunar dog is closely related to death. The lunar dog is a hunting dog, and it serves as an aid to cause the death of people, as in the legend of Actaeon.

The lunar dog is opposed to the shepherd dog. The universally accepted mythical function of the dog is that of psychopomp, a guide of the man on the night of death, after having been a companion during the day of the life.

All of these associations are linked to the invisible world and darkness, related to the sign where the Moon has its fall, Scorpio, and again this model is mixed with Persephone.

Hecate is the personification of the dark Moon, analogous to the feminine principle in its magnetic aspect. It symbolizes the terrible and castrating mother, causing madness, lunacy, and obsessions. The attributes of this feminine model are "the key," "the whip," "the dagger," and the "torch."

These attributes shed a little light on this dark and unknown archetype. When Demeter finds Hecate, she has a lit axe in her hands, constituting a symbol of purification. The symbolism of the torch tells us about a prototype that has undergone a purification, an illumination, or a profound transformation that gives it a special lucidity.

The "key" is a symbol of power, the key is used to open and close. The key symbolizes the boss, the master, the one who holds the power of decision and responsibility. The power of the key allows to unite and to divide, it is the power that allows access or encloses inside. From this symbolism, it can be deduced that this model can only be represented by a very special type of woman, who must demonstrate a very defined power of decision, a dominion, and a special responsibility. In esoteric language, possessing the key means having been initiated. It indicates not only the entrance to a place, city, or house, but also the entrance to a state, a spiritual dwelling, or an initiatory degree.

The "whip" is also a symbol of power. The symbolism of the whip merges the symbolism of the rope and the scepter, both signs of domination and superiority. The whip expresses the idea of punishment, and also the power to wrap and dominate. Therefore, this attribute indicates the power to punish, to do "justice". The right to inflict punishments is what best characterizes this lunar model, and has its best representation in the punishing, enveloping, and dominant woman.

The symbolism of the "dagger" also has a connotation of power, but in this case limited. The dagger cannot be assimilated to the sword in its meaning, since the possibility of being hidden is related to the longing for aggression, the unspoken, unconscious threat. The dagger is a servant of instincts, in the same way that the sword is of the spirit. The dagger, because of its size, denotes the "short" power of aggression, the lack of high aspirations, and superior power. The dagger represents a prototype with the power of aggression at "short distances", never in the light of day or the open. This power of aggression is what makes these women fearsome and respectable.

Symbolism of Mercury

Mercury is the first planet in our solar system.

It is best observed as a "morning star" during autumn and as an "evening star" in spring. However, there are six periods each year when it is well placed in the sky for observation.

These periods occur when the planet is at its maximum distance east or west of the Sun. These positions are known as elongations. During these periods, which last for one to two weeks, Mercury is visible for about an hour in the morning or evening sky. It then appears as a first magnitude "star," varying its brightness between Aldebaran and Sirius.

If you have the opportunity to look at it closely, you will easily be able to observe its characteristic orange color, and if you use a good telescope, you can observe its phases, very similar to those of the Moon.

In symbolic language, the color orange is considered the color of communication through words. It also represents the color of love between friends and comrades.

The orange color symbolizes the point of balance between spirit and sexuality. – Halfway between the yellow of the Sun and the red of Mars.

Mercury stages its influence as a duality. Mercury retains the meanings of the Sun – a symbol of Unity – and the Moon – multiplicity – it combines them and forms a new particular expression. Mercury communicates, connects, and associates the conscious mind – the Sun – with the unconscious – the Moon – for this reason astrologically influences thought and communication.

Mercury, being the planet closest to the Sun, is related to the level of consciousness closest to the Ego, that is, the mind, and the intellect.

The phases of the planet Mercury, similar to those of the Moon, correspond to the multiple and changing, symbolizing the variability of thought and the versatility of words.

This double nature of Mercury is repeated in all its descriptions. On the one hand, Mercury is considered feminine, as a "Yin" element, passive. It is the "quicksilver" or "liquid silver", that is, a typically lunar white metal.

On the other hand, it is masculine, it represents the active principle "Yang", the semen, the concentration of solar energy. It is the closest thing to the Sun, the thing that most influences the Sun, like mercury that dissolves gold.

In mythology, Hermes or Mercury maintains lunar legends. "Like Hecate, he is often represented with three heads, triform. He also has the condition of divinity of the roads, (the possibilities). He is the god of travel and receives honors at the crossroads like Hecate." However, in the legends, he acquires by donation, exchange, or directly by theft, solar attributes.

In classical mythology, Hermes for the Greeks or Mercury for the Romans is clearly distinguished from the rest of the gods. In his legend, it is said that, from his earliest childhood he showed his extraordinary ingenuity and his mischievous character.

Jumping furtively from his crib, he headed for the mountains where Apollo (the Sun) grazed his sacred herd of cows, separated from him the fifty best, and took them away, sheltered by the night, making them march backward, and to avoid being caught, he took the precaution, with his lively ingenuity, to disguise his footprints by wearing huge sandals made of branches that he cut and made.

Before locking the cows in a cave, he chose two, the ones that seemed the fattest to him; by rubbing laurel branches (solar symbol), he roasted their fatty parts, which he divided into twelve lots, one for each of the main gods of Olympus. (Including himself among them already).

Afterward, he returned to his home by entering through the keyhole and returned to his crib. The next day, Apollo realized the disappearance of his cows and, as he possessed the gift of clairvoyance, he went directly to Hermes' house, who stubbornly denied the theft. Apollo took him in his arms and took him to Olympus to present him before the courts, but on the way, guessing his weak point, he flattered him and managed to exchange his valuable caduceus for a lyre, which he made in an instant with a tortoise shell. (Since then, Apollo became the god of music and Hermes the protector of the flocks).

But the story doesn't end there; when they arrived in the presence of Zeus, the lord, and judge of the gods could not contain his laughter when he saw the cunning of the youngest of his offspring. But as he felt great affection for Apollo, he extracted from Hermes the promise that he would return his sacred cows.

Hermes' pranks were numerous. It is said that he was barely born when he knocked Eros down by tripping him and stole his quiver and love arrows. In a moment of carelessness, he stole the sword from the furious Ares; the trident from Artemis, the girdle from Aphrodite, and the scepter from Zeus himself, whom he also tried to steal the lightning bolt, but he burned himself and could not take it. For these crimes he was thrown out of Olympus, going to live in Thessaly, south of Mount Olympus, where he dedicated himself to shepherding and protecting thieves and merchants.

Despite his malicious and mischievous character, Hermes won the sympathy of the immortals, for he possessed a helpfulness and a fine wit that made him an effective assistant. Zeus eventually forgave him and made him his messenger. Since then, he has been considered the messenger of the gods.

Hermes was also a benefactor of humans; he protected the flocks, guided travelers, protected trade, and exchange, and inspired harmonious words and eloquent speeches in the human mind.

He also reached his influence on the underworld and it was he who guided the souls of the deceased to their final resting place. – He also maintains similarities with Hecate here –.

Hermes from the Greeks came to be called Mercury for the Romans, this new name is related to "merx", merchandise, and with "mercari", to traffic, being this the name that they bequeathed us and that is used today.

However, the cult of Mercury has been maintained in our Mediterranean culture, although with certain transformations. Thus, within Catholic mythology, its survival is evident through the centuries.

It is possible to identify him among the icons and saints of the Catholic Church. Throughout the northern Mediterranean basin, in any traditional business, from Thessaloniki in Greece to Cádiz in Spain, you can see an icon or image of the god of commerce, although he is now known by another name. In the Spanish Levant, he is recognized under the name of Saint Pancras, an omnipresent image in all classical businesses.

On the esoteric or occult (hermetic) plane, Mercury is related to the transmutation of internal energies. In one of his legends, Hermes interposes the golden rod he exchanged with Apollo, between two snakes fighting each other, which coiled around the staff forming the caduceus, Mercury's main attribute.

The secret of the meaning of the symbol of the staff is that it represents the spinal cord, with the two snakes being the two main forces, the duality manifested by the force of life and the force of nature.

Both forces fight for supremacy in each human being. One tries to externalize itself through procreation, while the other struggles to free itself and evolve by transcending the physical body. (These forces or channels are not of a psychic type and have nothing to do with the organic elements that make up the body).

The famous alchemical mercury, to be transmuted into gold, is another way of referring to that same internal battle that liberates the forces of consciousness from the dominion of the material physical.

Mercury manifests itself both in the world of the living and the world of the dead, representing the umbilical cord, the "silver cord" that unites the physical organism, dependent on the laws of Saturn (time and matter) with the universe free of time.

In such a way those who have experienced the state of trans corporal consciousness or "out of body" according to American psych terminology, will remember that in that state that layer of mercurial consciousness that reasons, that level of thought that precisely will make the return to the physical body possible.

The ancient initiates in the Eleusinian mysteries knew the experience of this "journey" to the beyond, for which they named Mercury as the only or last guide.

If we transfer the astrological influence of Mercury to the human consciousness, it corresponds, by analogy, to the level of consciousness that allows us to nuance, count, measure, weigh, and take notes of any kind.

The influence of Mercury is staged through intellect, understanding, argumentation, and everything that makes communication possible.

Mercury makes its influence felt in each of us through logic, ingenuity, and manual skills of all kinds, from writing to the manufacture or use of all kinds of utensils. It is therefore related to writings, letters, messages, correspondence, merchandise, etc.

As we have seen, it is Mercury who is responsible for matters related to commerce, contracts, deals, business, traffic, dealings, etc. This is why it is related to merchants, merchants, brokers, dealers, store clerks, guides, administrators, students, artisans, and thieves.

Mercury, in each of us, is in full activity in the actions of expressing; like what is happening now, to manifest verbally or in writing, to say, to speak, to formulate, to expose, and to have an opinion.

The influence of Mercury is staged as cunning, sagacity, stratagems, tricks, ruses, and tricks, and it can be associated with "knowing how to swim and keep your clothes on", "knowing Latin", being cunning, fine, mischievous, rogue, etc.

In the field of actions or events, it is related to everything that involves exchange and movement, all kinds of communications or dissemination. It also has to do with short trips and displacements.

Mercury has preferred places to manifest its influence, such as bookstores, shops, craft workshops, schools, institutes, and all places close to which we travel periodically.

In the human organism, it makes its influence felt in all elongated cells, such as neurons, (nerves), spinal cord, intervertebral discs, ligaments, tendons, bronchial tree, intestines, etc.

When the energy of Mercury cannot be manifested through communication, which usually happens with tense transits of Saturn, when the flow of Mercury is cut off or its manifestation is difficult, then there is a tendency to somatize or become ill in these parts of the body.

This is confirmed by people who were born with the Sun in Gemini or Mercury or Venus in Gemini, who are affected by the bronchi or ligaments, while those who are related to Virgo are affected by the intestines or intervertebral discs.

On the other hand, it is notable the number of deaths of famous writers, purely mercurial, due to the deterioration of the bronchial tree.

The pure model of a mercurial person is difficult to find, but it is generally revealed by a thin body and face, a fairly prominent forehead, the nose is always elongated, the eyes have an air of inquiry and are very mobile, the lips are very thin, the hands are thin and expressive, and the chin is quite small.

These are people who gesture a lot. In dealing with them, it is clear that they have something to say about everything, and we will see them making games of wit and observe that they have a good argument.

Mercury has its Domicile in the zodiac sign of Gemini and Virgo, where it also has its Exaltation, the Detriment in Pisces, the Fall in Pisces, the Joy in the 1st House, and the Sadness in the 7th House.

Age of Mercury

Mercury has more influence, is stronger, more important, and is much more noticeable from 4 to 14 years old.

Ben Ragel says that this time it strengthens its understanding, speech, and reasoning. It is in this stage of life that the person receives most of their information.

In reality, the astrological age of Mercury coincides fully with the age of compulsory schooling in most countries of the world. A child learns a language much faster than an adult.

In this time, the person comes into contact with the foundations of science, knowledge, skills, mastery, and everything that can be learned. It will be understood that the most important information is the information that is received in these ages.

The age of Mercury is a time of intellectual development. It is a stage in life when it is necessary to recognize, memorize, and organize words and ideas.

During these years, the intellect is much more vigorous, the ability to retain information is greater, and the left hemisphere of the brain, where the language area is located, associated with the planet Mercury, is much more active. It is the time of learning, when a whole series of very complex codes are integrated that are the summary of the experience of many generations of humans.

A 12-year-old child born in the 21st century could be considered a wise man in the 9th century. Despite this, the period of learning tends to increase, since human knowledge, the information that is needed to understand even moderately the information circulating in the world of this 21st century, is always greater. Therefore, the time of Mercury is also extended and enters times or ages that were previously exclusively of the next planet.

Keywords for Mercury

Character Destiny

Ingenious communication, oral or written

Sharp exchanges of all kinds

Skilled studies, accounting, or finance

Ocurrent blood relatives, siblings

Indecisive young people, children, son

Eloquent short trips

Waggish business in general

Calculating intelligence

Symbolism of Venus

Venus is the second planet in our solar system.

It is the brightest star after the Sun and the Moon, and it is very similar in size to Earth.

From an astronomical point of view, Venus, like the Moon, appears to the observer with different degrees of brightness, because it also has phases. Additionally, sometimes it appears on the horizon before sunrise, sometimes it is only visible at sunset, and for several months each year, it disappears from visual observation due to its relative proximity to the Sun.

In astrology, we also consider some vibratory variants of Venus, both in quantity and quality, depending in this case on its location in the different zodiac signs, which we call domiciles or exaltations of the planet, places where its effects are expressed with greater clarity, independence, freedom, and purity.

In addition, meanings are also extracted from the three ways in which it appears to the observer. When it is oriental and is observed before sunrise, when it is occidental and is observed in the early hours of the night, and when it is not observed due to its proximity to the Sun.

To delve into astrological interpretation, it is convenient to know how Venus influences.

Venus, like the Moon, is primarily staged in the realm of feelings and is expressed in affections of all kinds, sympathies, and romantic sentimentalism that leads to the enjoyment of the senses or carnal love.

Venus is the only planet (except the Sun and the Moon) that can cause an eclipse of Mercury, that is, it can interpose itself between the intellect, hide it, and temporarily nullify it.

For this reason, when the romantic influence of the planet Venus "possesses" us temporarily, we do or say things that go beyond the reasonable, and the intelligent, in those moments, in which we are captive of Venus, all trace of reason is annulled, as happens to us when we are in love.

Something similar happens when humor or fun appears. When we tell a joke, we start with something logical, Mercury, until we break or annul the reasonable, and then the funny, Venus, appears.

An excess of Venus causes situations in which we are laughing so hard that we can't breathe. Curiously, recent discoveries about the surface of Venus indicate that the temperature produced by the greenhouse effect of its sulfurous clouds creates an environment so warm that lead would melt.

Lead is associated with Saturn. By analogy, it can be said that the influence of Venus melts sadness, ends sorrows, ends restrictive situations and hardships, and dilutes social impediments or conditioning and material demands. As happens during festivals and celebrations.

No matter how poor a town or people are, when their "festivals" arrive, poverty ends, at least for those days.

Venus, along with the Moon, completes the feminine nature of women, adding to fertility and the instinct of protection, grace, delicacy, and charm, which makes women attractive, striking, captivating, and desirable.

When a woman wears tight pink clothes, she is building a bridge for the goddess Venus to pass through her and fulfill her function of seducing and charming.

Venus is closely related to the feminine polarity of consciousness and is associated with the ability to seduce, such as when one gently persuades others, flatters them, attracts them, or sweetly captivates them.

For the ancient Greeks, the gods could possess us. The possession of Venus can be noticed as a change of mood like a heart flip and blushing. It is always perceived at a personal level as a disturbing and pleasant disturbance that alters consciousness, nullifies reason, and moves to tenderness and love.

Venus, due to its multiple natures, is also related to the feeling of pity and tenderness that is felt for the misfortune or evil of others. Venus encourages almsgiving and aid to the needy; for this reason, it is analogous to charity, compassion, and love for one's neighbor.

On another level, Venus is analogous to the impulse that the will receives to use materials, images, or sounds that express its perceptions, fantastic or real, with the purpose of pleasing, delighting, or fascinating others, at the same time that it makes us aware of the artistic manifestations made by others. It is the sense of aesthetics, the appreciation of beauty and harmony. -Spanish words such as venustez, venustidad, or venusto are still preserved to define perfect or very graceful beauty. -

Through Venus, a subtle oscillation in human consciousness is filtered that affects social behavior vividly; Venus corresponds to attention and respect in dealing with others; good manners, kindness, compliments, protocol, and urbanity that can be observed in the acts of "giving way," "giving up the seat," or greeting. Saying "Hello!", raising a hand in a sign of calling, gracefully claiming the attention of others, etc., can be considered small Venusian effluvia.

The same influence of Venus induces us to groom ourselves, and it is not manifested exclusively in women; in men, it leads them to shave, beautify themselves, perfume themselves, and dress with composure to enhance their attractiveness. An excess of Venus in men, as you know, makes them effeminate and more graceful.

Venus and her symbolic white dove represent peace, harmony, and tranquility, as well as all kinds of peaceful festivals, where fun, recreation, entertainment, invitations, dances, parties, and pilgrimages appear. That is why it is linked to treats, offerings, invitations, ceremonies, and gifts.

As with any force subjected to multiplicity, Venus also has its negative connotations. It is responsible for laziness, idleness, inaction, laziness, strikes, and indolence.

Venus also symbolizes poison and is associated with venereal diseases and spells or enchantments. Venus especially influences places that are related to decorations, works of art, or beauty, such as art galleries, beauty salons, fashion stores, dance halls, and festive centers, etc.

In terms of people, it is related to young and beautiful women, artists, decorators, stylists, fashion designers, and all those who stand out for their attractiveness or who dedicate themselves to promoting beauty and harmony.

The pure human model that Venus represents is of a rather small, graceful, and well-proportioned body, with a face that is almost always rounded, a round and fleshy nose at the tip, rather elegant, a small well-arched mouth, with a beautiful design, the lower lip somewhat thicker than the upper lip, a round chin a little greasy, lively ways, sweet eyes, and graceful gestures.

As in the case of the other planets, when the energy of Venus is activated, it will first try to manifest itself through a pattern of behavior, a way of being, adopting an appearance by this planet, which implies deploying a humorous, cheerful, pious, peaceful, romantic, seductive, or artistic disposition.

When we are not able to "interpret" or channel this type of energy through ourselves, it can be done by projecting it onto the image of another person in our immediate surroundings, such as a partner, daughters, female characters, artists, or people who awaken sympathy, joy, or love, through whom it is projected or channeled and this energy of Venus is allowed to flow.

In case we do not have the mood or the right people, the energy of Venus can flow or be channeled through the pantry, the fridge, the money box, well-decorated rooms, game rooms, festive places, vacation centers, play, leisure or fun, places that are cheerful and beautiful, such as gardens, dance halls, beauty or fashion centers, etc.

When the energy of Venus is unable to flow through any of the previous channels, like the other planets, it has an area or organ of the body through which it can flow as a final sink.

The organ or part of the body with which it is related can experience negative effects on the planet if its expression at higher levels has been unduly hindered and has not been able to flow.

In the human organism, this occurs with the throat, ears, kidneys, female reproductive system, and the prostate in men.

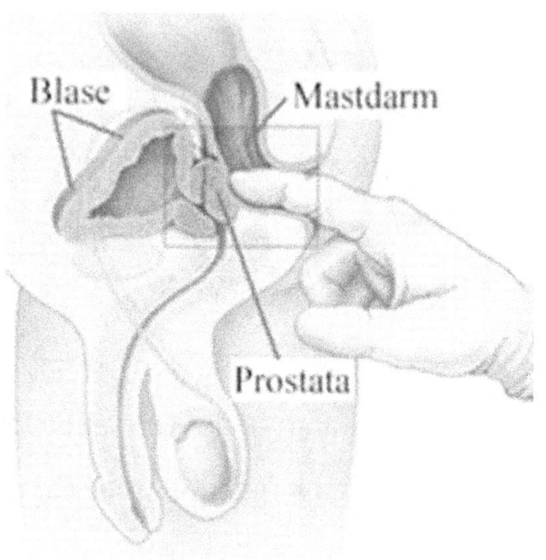

When these areas of the body are affected by some disease, it is a symptom that they have not known how to give vent to their romantic impulses, or that they have yielded to social blackmail and have neglected love.

Venus has its Domicile in the zodiac signs of Taurus and Libra, its Exaltation in Pisces, its Exile in Virgo, its Fall in Virgo, its Joy in the Fifth House, and its Sadness in the Eleventh House.

Age of Venus

Venus and her model of behavior are expressed much better in the age that corresponds to her, which is from 15 to 24 years old. The French call this age "la bouté du diable" (the beauty of the devil) and in beauty contests they admit candidates just up to that same age.

Pure beauty is more noticeable at that age. No matter how beautiful a woman is, she is more beautiful or seductive at that age, and the same happens with a man, in the sense of a "Danone" man.

Ben Ragel says that during this period the spirit of the born shows itself despotic, bearing badly that his will is not obeyed. He becomes amorous and is attracted to beautiful appearances and fornication; he deceives himself and blinds himself to any event of this nature that occurs to them.

Keywords of Venus

Character Destiny

Compassionate parties and gifts

Deceptive situations of recreation and fun

Persuasive romantic loves

Courteous affective demonstrations

Flattering flattery and bribes

Funny artists, young women or girls

Attractive artistic or aesthetic expressions

Indolent rests, peace, and truce

Objects and Places

Copper objects

Art objects

Ornaments of all kinds

Pocket money

Art galleries

Beauty salons

Warm and humid places

Festive centers

The Deity of Venus

Venus, as a deity, that is, as a luminous and celestial being that influences human behavior from the collective unconscious in the form of an archetype or model to imitate, manifests itself in cultures of all times as a divine model that receives worship through different versions, different names, and diverse origins, but always unequivocally referred to the planet Venus.

The exalted model of Venus, Venus in its phase of maximum luminosity, when the planet is oriental because the atmosphere is always cleaner in the morning is related to Venus in its exaltation of the zodiac sign of Pisces where they have dignity, is represented mythologically by a woman, almost a girl, with alabaster-white skin, of perfect beauty, who emerges from the Sea (Pisces). Born from the foamy marine mixture and the creative power of the sky.

Hesiod recounted it as follows: Resting on the softest, luminous, and iridescent mother-of-pearl of a splendid seashell that served as her ship, bed and cradle, and blown by the sweet Zephyr (the moist wind), she reached the coast where she was received by the Hours, who, amazed and absorbed by so much beauty, made her advance still dripping with salt water that did not want to end, so as not to abandon that perfect body.

Wrapped in the incomparable splendor of her beauty and adorned better than with the richest finery with her virginal and noble nudity, the Hours only placed a necklace around her neck and a crown of flowers on her head, and led her to the palace of the gods of Olympus. All of them were amazed by her extraordinary beauty and charm. With a slight smile on her lips, all the immortals were conquered.

This staging of Venus is the exaltation of beauty, the exaltation of Venus, which on the other hand, her birth in the sea leads us back to Pisces.

In her legends, it is also said that as she was born in the sea, which had been so kind to her, she could not show ingratitude to Neptune, lord, and master of the liquid marine element, and she yielded to his humble entreaties, and accepted him as a lover.

The second model of Venus, the one that represents the planet when it is observed at sunset, described by the ancient mythologists, appears, among other representations, as Ishtar of Assyria, an ancient representation of the planet Venus.

This deity of the planet Venus enters the scene of the myth as a warrior divinity, at the same time as the goddess of love. Married to Ashur (Ares, Mars), she accompanied her husband on his warlike expeditions, "covered in combat and clothed in terror."

She was represented on a chariot pulled by seven lions and carrying a bow in her hands. The seven lions pulling the celestial chariot symbolize the creative and ordering power of the seventh zodiac sign, that is, Libra or the seventh House, the area of competitors and rivals, and marriage. On the other hand, the bow speaks to us of the masculine principle of this model. (Libra is a masculine sign)

The bow has an arrow, and the arrow always has a phallic, male meaning, because the arrow penetrates; by shooting, Love, son of Venus, exercises his role of fertilization.

The symbolism of the bow also leads us to the representation of the middle phases of the planet, showing the duality of light and darkness. In this symbolic scheme, the Masculine and the Feminine appear in a solid embrace. Venus, love, serves as their platform and the scale represents the balance between these two natural forces.

Another representation of Venus in Libra, with masculine attributes, is found in Greek culture, where she appears under the name of Ourania.

The muse of astrology.

The attributes and objects with which the deity of Venus-Urania is presented will clarify its symbolic content a bit more. In some representations, she carries a scepter in one hand and an apple in the other.

The scepter is a masculine and phallic symbol, it extends the arm and means power and authority. The scepter of the Egyptian goddesses was a symbol of the joy that the pleasure of being able to execute their wills provided. In other words, in plain language, the scepter symbolizes the pleasure of doing what you want. −Classic pleasure of all people born with the Sun in Libra.

The symbol of the scepter gradually evolves until it becomes a fleur−de−lis, but maintains the same symbolic meaning. The fleur−de−lis is valued not for the flower but for the elongated rhizomes of the plant from which an essential oil is extracted with which an aphrodisiac perfume is created twenty times more expensive than a rose. Its soft aroma of old wood and violets upsets the sense of logic and moves love. This perfume was the favorite of the Medici women, who reigned in Florence in the 13th century and Spain centuries later.

On the other hand, the apple is a feminine symbol that has several interpretations; on the one hand, it represents earthly desires and their unleashing.

The prohibition of eating the apple came from the supreme voice that opposes the exaltation of material desires.

The thirst for knowledge is, as Nietzsche said, a zone only intermediate between earthly desires and pure and true spirituality, therefore the apple has a deeper and hidden symbolism, where the symbol comes from what the apple has inside. A five-pointed star, which can be seen when cutting an apple perpendicularly to the axis in two, formed by the alveoli that enclose the seeds, appears as the traditional symbol of knowledge. (Dictionary of Symbols, by Chevalier.)

In later representations, it appears with the scepter and the apple fused into a single symbol; the hand mirror, the magic mirror that grants knowledge of things past and future.

The word "mirror" comes from the Latin word "epeculum", from which the word "speculate" also comes. Originally, to speculate meant to observe the sky and the movements of the stars.

The ancient practitioners of Astrology, or the art of Venus-Urania, used circular mirrors to make their observations. They did not look directly at the sky. Something similar happens today, where astrologers do not look directly at the sky, but use that magic mirror that we now call the astrological mandala or natal chart.

In another sense, to speculate means to meditate and reflect; linking us again with the symbolism of knowledge, of the five-pointed star. The pentagram, as it is also called, always accompanies this model of Venus-Urania, Muse of Astrology, ruler of Libra, a masculine, cardinal, and air sign, mobile as thought, free as the wind, and with the same freedom of action as the ancient Egyptian goddesses.

Perhaps that is why astrologers, influenced by this archetype, are people who are difficult to indoctrinate or submit to the wills of others. All of them, including you, for reading this, maintain the tendency to do what they want.

The third model of Venus corresponds to its domicile in the zodiac sign of Taurus, the sign of the domicile of Venus, and where the Moon has its exaltation.

Here she appears as "Venus Genitrix", Venus's mother. In these representations, she always appears with an apple in one hand and a baby in swaddling clothes in the other. The child replaces the masculine symbol, the scepter, the fleur-de-lis, or the mirror. She is presented riding in a chariot drawn by white doves and two doves are always perched by her side.

The dove is the sacred bird of Venus, it was the gift of lovers and a symbol of peace and love. As an attribute, she has a girdle, which symbolizes bondage and fidelity and describes functions that require dedication and loyalty.

The girdle of Venus contains all sorts of enchantments, Hesiod and Homer describe it as a divine talisman that confers on women an irresistible power.

The girdle is also associated with the crown or the diadem, and in the modern representation of this divinity, it appears crowned with flowers and dressed as the mantle of the flowering spring that it presides over.

The dove, the flowery white of her clothing, the goddess of love, the feast of spring, art, and joy, all these expressions lead us to the "White Dove" of Andalusian spring, with her dress of white flowers and her child in swaddling clothes.

The son of Venus is Love, and this remains the same in all traditions of all times and places.

In the Holy Scriptures, it is also possible to detect an identification between the son of Venus and Christ, which reaches the point of manifesting that intimate relationship. In Revelation 21:16, it is written:

"I, Jesus, have sent my angel to you to give you this testimony for the churches. I am the Root and the Offspring of David, **and the Bright and Morning Star."**

Was not the message of Jesus, "Love one another"? This message of love corresponds to the exaltation of Venus in Pisces. During this Piscean Age, this message has always been latent.

Symbolism of Mars

Mars is the first outer planet from Earth. When viewed with the naked eye, when its brightness is most pronounced, it surpasses all other planets except Venus, with which it is compared as its opposite and complementary.

The planet Mars is a primary competitor among planets for biological development.

It shines with an orange light, the color of burning embers or coals with shades ranging from yellow to red. Because of this reddish or bloody color, the ancients associated it with the god of war.

In astrology, the planet Mars is associated with the color red. Red is the color of fiery and vibrant senses, passion, and activity.

Applying the main axiom of symbolism, which states that all manifestation is dual, we can say that there are two symbolisms of red, just as there are two symbolisms of Mars.

The first red is feminine, has a power of attraction, is centripetal and dark, and represents the magnetic aspect of Mars. It corresponds to the nocturnal red, the red of the central fire of the human being and the Earth, the color of the soul, libido, and heart. It is also the color of esoteric knowledge, forbidden to the uninitiated, and that the wise conceal beneath their mantle. This feminine red is the matrix red. (The mother goddess of India is represented in this red color). This dark, initiatory, and centripetal red also contains a funerary image (the red of Scorpio). The color purple is related to death; it is the color of blood that when spilled signifies death.

The other red, associated with the luminosity of the planet and its domicile in Aries, is close to white and gold and becomes masculine and solar. It constitutes the essential symbol of vital force. It embodies ardor, impulsive and generous force, and free and triumphant Eros.

Tribes in Africa and America paint themselves with red paint, as they believe it stimulates vital forces and awakens desire. This red is always an exciting color, it incites passion.

Mandrills and other animals have red erogenous zones. Women have used it throughout history to excite men; red dresses, red lips, etc.

The astrological influence of the planet Mars is present in everything red or hot.

We can detect the influence of the planet Mars in situations of turmoil and confused movement or agitation in people.

Mars can be perceived as noises and rumors caused by people when they are excited in tumults.

When the influence of Mars is very intense, situations of "hot blood" are staged, states of alteration, irritation, and excitement that usually end in violence.

The astrological influence of the planet Mars has a lot to do with enthusiasm, stimulation, invigoration, the desire to live, and optimism.

In another sense, Mars is responsible for competitions, races, sports in general, and martial arts, and determines the competitive aspirations of each person.

Therefore, it is responsible for boldness, daring, recklessness, and courage, and is related to dynamic decisions and rushed actions.

Mars is analogous to the determination to continue, the ease, boldness, and action, therefore it always synchronizes with situations of energy consumption. The energy of Mars is self-assertive and is expressed in moments of "speaking clearly", of throwing it in the middle of the street, of going against the wind and the tide, going blindly.

The influence of Mars is present in us when the "I have to survive" appears, when life feels threatened, representing the struggle for conservation.

At an individual level, Mars is perceived as agitation, palpitations, shaking, or chills and is associated with states of agitation, alteration, irritation, and ignitions. It is the focus of consciousness that feels like ardor, and rapture, and that is always present in orgasm.

In its most positive aspect, the resonances of Mars pull us out of any depression, make us venture out again, and tempt us to approve fortune. It can also be associated with the vocational impulse.

Mars has a lot to do with courage, effort, encouragement, and spirit. It is evident in people who have a will of iron, and who are effective in their work with good decision-making skills, initiative, and great dexterity.

In contrast, unbalanced or weak Mars energies are perceived in people as a source of decreased sexual appetite, lack of dynamism, discouragement, depression, and deterioration in vocational impulse. This is reflected in work as a decrease or lack of work attention, and difficulty in decision-making, and is the cause of distractions, carelessness, negligence, fatigue, lassitude, discouragement, and fatigue. Its weakness is the cause of most accidents.

That is why Mars is always associated with accidents.

Mars is associated with places where tumults, struggles, or confrontations take place, such as the ring of a boxing ring, football stadiums, racing circuits, etc. It also corresponds to hot and dry places, such as furnaces and foundries.

In its negative aspect, the influence of Mars corresponds to cruelty, anger, and brutality. It can also be associated with envy, revenge, and savagery.

In people, this negative aspect of Mars is perceived as "having a bad stomach," "having no scruples," behaving cruelly and being soulless or ferocious. People marked by this negative aspect of Mars play the role of "bully," "tough guy," "gangster," "hooligan," "fighter," and "troublemaker." These individuals attract the negative effluvia of Mars, producing uproars, challenges, brawls, and skirmishes.

The collective influence of Mars is staged in major sporting events, where attendees, possessed by the influence of Mars, become brutish, insulting, and shouting like true savages.

About people, Mars is analogous to military personnel, police officers, athletes, surgeons, etc. The pure model has a strong physical appearance but is not very tall, with dark or lively eyes that fix their gaze on the interlocutor, arched eyebrows, an aquiline nose, thin lips, a well-defined chin, an always muscular body, and a strong voice.

In the human body, Mars rules the muscles, and the head, and is related to red blood cells.

Keywords –to use in elemental interpretation:

Tireless

Boisterous

Choleric

Daring

Abrupt

Naive

Optimistic

Unthinking

Concepts for General Interpretation:

Dynamic decisions and rash actions: This concept refers to situations in which a person or character makes quick, decisive decisions without taking the time to carefully consider all the options. This can be seen as a positive or negative trait, depending on the context. In some cases, it can be seen as a sign of decisiveness and courage. In other cases, it can be seen as a sign of impulsiveness or recklessness.

Energy-consuming situations: This concept refers to situations that require a lot of physical or mental energy. This could include activities such as sports, work, or combat. It could also include situations that are emotionally or mentally demanding.

Competitive aspirations: This concept refers to the desire to win or be the best. This could be seen in sports, business, or any other area of life. Competitive aspirations can be a positive force, motivating people to achieve their goals. However, they can also be a negative force, leading to conflict or aggression.

Vocational drive: This concept refers to the desire to find a meaningful career. This could be driven by a passion for a particular field, a desire to make a difference in the world, or simply a need to earn a living. Vocational drive can be a powerful motivator, helping people to achieve their goals.

Sexual or life instinct: This concept refers to the basic instinct to survive and reproduce. This is a powerful force that can drive people to make decisions that are not always rational. The sexual or life instinct can be seen in many different areas of life, including relationships, careers, and even hobbies.

Struggle for conservation: This concept refers to the effort to protect oneself or one's resources. This could be seen in situations of physical danger, such as a fight or a natural disaster. It could also be seen in situations of emotional or psychological danger, such as a relationship conflict or a job loss. The struggle for conservation can be a very intense experience, leading people to make decisions that they would not normally make.

Relationships with doctors, dentists, etc.: This concept refers to the way people interact with people in positions of authority, such as doctors, dentists, or teachers. These relationships can be complex and challenging, as they often involve issues of trust and vulnerability. The way people interact with authority figures can reveal a lot about their personalities and values.

Athletes, military, strong men: This concept refers to people who are physically or mentally strong. These people are often seen as role models, and they can represent ideals of strength, courage, and determination. The presence of athletes, military personnel, or other strong men in a work of art or literature can be seen as a way of exploring themes of power, conflict, and identity.

Mythology of Mars

In Babylon, he was represented as Ashur, in Greece as Ares, and in Rome, he was known as Mars.

Ashur was the national god of the Assyrians, he was considered the creator of heaven and hell, author of all humans, lord of all gods, and in charge of fixing destiny. His name means "benevolent".

But Ashur was above all a warlike god who shared the warlike instincts of the Assyrian people. He followed his army into battle, fought alongside them, took care that his soldiers did not miss their shots, and always favored them with victory.

Ashur was represented in the form of a winged disk, or floating in the air, and also had the function of protector of fertility. Then he was represented surrounded by branches and his symbol was a goat.

The goat is a symbol of a taste for spontaneous freedom; from the root goat, caprice comes. This symbol of the goat is associated with its exaltation in the zodiac sign of Capricorn. This model of Mars in Capricorn has a relatively modern symbolic expression in the Arcanum number four of the Tarot, in which it appears with the image of the Emperor. As in all his representations, he is seated, forming a four with the crossing of his legs, on a cubic stone, and the mountains representing Capricorn in the background.

In his hands and as attributes he carries a scepter with a sphere with a cross upwards, an unmistakable symbol of Mars. The scepter is a phallic and masculine symbol, it extends the arm and is a sign of power and authority. (House X, Capricorn) The cube on which he is seated symbolizes material perfection. It is the image of eternity, because of its non-spiritual character, and represents the idea of solidity and permanence. For all this, this first model of Mars is associated with its exaltation in Capricorn.

For the Greeks, this archetype awakens more fear than sympathy. Ares is here the god of war, of blind and brutal courage, of thirst for blood and destruction. "Of all the gods who inhabit Olympus," says Ares to Zeus of the Iliad, "you are the most hateful to me; for you only love disputes, discord, war, and combat; you have the intractable and unruly character of your mother Hera, whom I can barely restrain with my words."

As the god of war that he was, he naturally sought his solace in combat. Mounted on a chariot drawn by two horses, or in the company of his two servants (satellites), Deimos (terror) and Phobos (terror), he left behind devastation and death.

This model of Mars is perfectly represented in Tarot card number seven, where he appears mounted on his chariot, drawn by his two horses, leaving behind the devastated city; this is the representation of Mars in the Fall, of Mars in Cancer, of Mars hated and weak.

In Greek mythology, this weak model of Mars was almost always defeated by his opponents; Athena surpasses him in combat with her greater intelligence; Hephaestus defeated him when he went in search of him and another puts him in a ridiculous situation; Heracles defeated him in combat; Diomedes wounds him and he had to return to Olympus groaning and the Aloades chained him.

This model of Mars or Ares symbolizes brute force that gets drunk with its size, weight, speed, noise, and destructive capacity and mocks justice, measure, and humanity. This model comes to represent the cultural model of the United States, a country where the most brutal prevails and where warriors are still worshiped after one of their raids.

Mars, however, is the quintessential Roman god. His cult surpasses that of Jupiter. Although it was identified with the Greek Ares, it already existed at the beginning of Roman mythology; first for being the father of Romulus; according to tradition, and then for its functions as the god of agriculture and war. This model corresponds perfectly with the successive stages of the Roman citizen; first a farmer, then a warrior, and after the victory, with the claim of lands, again a farmer. Here the model of Mars represents the force of spring that breaks with its head on the Earth's crust to see the light. It is Mars in its domicile of Aries. It is the force of the ram first, and then the force of the plow.

The ram symbolizes penetration and ambivalent force, fertility, and destruction. The plow also symbolizes penetration and force, destruction, and fertilization. In the Aryan legend of Rama, this hero marries Sita (the furrow in the field). Being the earth a feminine element, its action symbolizes the mentioned union.

The last cult with him was honored by the Romans, he received him as the god of spring, and his feasts were celebrated with the Sun in Aries, at that time the month of March bears his name.

In the traditional representation, Mars always appears as a warrior armed with a spear and sword and with a helmet on his head, sometimes he usually wears armor but leaves his chest free as a symbol of boldness and courage. (Chestless).

The spear has a symbolic content of axis and can be summarized as a sacrifice, although it is also a warrior and sexual symbol. The symbolism of the sword has different allegories, since from the Middle Ages it is associated with the cross. But in a primary sense, it is a simultaneous symbol of the wound and the power to wound, therefore it is a sign of freedom and strength.

In alchemy, the sword symbolizes the purifying fire. The saber cuts through the healthy, is a weapon of decision, and is the instrument of the acting truth, it is a symbol of the lucid force of the mind that dares to cut the problem.

The helmet is a symbol of concealment, invulnerability, and power. (We will reserve the concept of invisibility for the helmet of Pluto). The helmet of Mars, which always carries some type of ornament, be it feathers, plumes, or plant elements, is a symbol of protection of thoughts, but also of concealment of intentions.

Symbolism of Jupiter

Jupiter is the largest planet in the solar system, with a mass greater than that of all the other planets combined. It has twelve moons, four of which are visible with a pair of binoculars; two of them, Callisto and Ganymede, are larger than the planet Mercury.

To understand Jupiter's astrological influence, we must consider it as one more focus of human consciousness. It can be associated with social identity, or what we are socially speaking. Its influence filters through moral conscience, and a sense of justice, and is the influence that leads us to sound judgment and condescension.

In another sense, the astrological influence of the planet Jupiter is staged in the authoritarian order that is imposed on us from the outside and corresponds to the law that governs us, the religion that has been imposed on us, and the power of justice, the imams and the inquisitors, therefore, at the individual level, it represents how the relationships with justice, religion, law or right are going to be.

The influence of the planet Jupiter, in a positive sense, is the staging of abundance, of wealth; in its manifestations, it is prodigal to satiety, it grants opulence and represents goods, big money, and capital.

Its presence is perceived in the stagings where there are achievements, successes, satisfactions, and abundance. It represents a comfortable life, supplied with everything necessary to have a good time with peace of mind, and its influence tends to generate peace and comfort.

Jupiter is openly perceived in states of satisfaction and comfort; it is the conscience of the rich, of the full of goods and it is noted as having the right to enjoyment, having reason, and is staged in the acts of achieving, winning, getting away with it and reaping benefits.

The position of Jupiter within a natal chart, tells us the sector of life in which each person has some concession that will free them from some burden and grant them some privilege. In general, it indicates the focus through which wealth and well-being will emanate.

The Jupiterian promiscuity manifests itself in the lives of the people on whom it influences the most, Sagittarians, Pisces, Cancer and those who have the planet angular, as a disordered appetite towards the delights of life, both carnal, -lust-, as in all kinds of excesses that pursue individual satisfaction, such as traveling to paradisiacal places to do nothing of profit, but simply enjoy, that is what is most noticeable of the influence of Jupiter.

It can be said that Jupiter is the "patron" of hedonism, which in case anyone does not know, is the doctrine that proclaims as the supreme end of life the achievement of pleasure. – Have you not met a Pisces with that attitude? – Covered in religiosity or mysticism of course!

The great sin to which the influence of Jupiter leads is the tendency to sleep too much and to neglect obligations, and laziness. Sagittarians and Pisces could produce much more but laziness and hedonism eat away at their morality

The influence of Jupiter is responsible for the love of the easy life and the impulses tending to waste money on unnecessary or superfluous whims.

The best or most pleasant stagings of the influence of Jupiter are related to prosperous situations and satisfactory events and are noticeable in the states of affability that make people affected by its influence appear kind, benevolent, expansive, cheerful, and inclined towards equity, justice, and good intentions.

"There is nothing more to see than the "posh" people or the "minding" travelers, who when they are on a tourist trip to Third World countries give some alms, they feel more religious and with good intentions, something that never happens to them in their town. That is because when we travel we are under the influence of Jupiter."

On the other hand, the negative influence of Jupiter, something that occurs especially when Jupiter is in a bad cosmic state or when it receives bad aspects, makes the person despotic, argumentative, joker, and impertinent, and also induces vain, sarcastic, intrusive and carefree behavior.

The influence of Jupiter is staged in places or sites of altitude, the elevated zones, with high or distant. Therefore it is associated with the exterior, the most distant or unknown, and the displacements towards this type of place, as well as the treatment of people of foreign origin or certain hierarchy, all those people who cause us admiration, such as certain types of foreigners, –it is a pity to say it, but we do not feel the same before a poor moor who comes in a dinghy as for a rich Arab from the Persian Gulf.– The Gulf is of Jupiter and the poor moor of Saturn. I'm sorry, I didn't invent it.

Clerics, jurists, professors, and all the "divas" that cause us admiration, whether in art or sport, also express well the influence of Jupiter. It is related to people or places that attract attention for their splendor, knowledge, or because they stand out in some way.

The influence of the planet Jupiter is also staged in admirable places that are an inexcusable tourist destination, such as churches, and also in stations, national highways, universities, etc.

Jupiter is tourism and everything related to it. It is only necessary to remember that Jupiter is the ruler of Spain and our country is one of the leading tourist powers in the world. Without tourism, Spain would be devoured by misery, in fact, Spain was in misery until tourism arrived.

Jupiter, as a representative of a person model, is associated with individuals of sound judgment, who offer security. The physical aspect of the pure model is of a large and well-formed body, tending to obesity, broad chest, high forehead, soft and well-spaced eyes, somewhat wavy hair, pink complexion, strong nose, pointed and rosy cheeks, with a certain paternalistic or benevolent attitude. The male prototype usually wears a well-groomed beard.

In the human body, it rules the liver and is related to the thighs of the legs and arms, the ribs, the circulatory system, the cheekbones of the face, and the left ear.

Jupiter is in its Domicile in the signs of Sagittarius and Pisces, it is exalted in the sign of Cancer, in its Joy in the 11th house, exiled in Virgo and Gemini, in Fall in Capricorn and its sadness in the 5th house. The age at which the influence of Jupiter flows most naturally is 56 years old.

Specifically, Jupiter Is Associated with the Following:

Expansion: Jupiter is a planet of growth and expansion. It represents our capacity for growth, both physically and spiritually. It also represents our ability to expand our horizons and explore new possibilities.

Fortune: Jupiter is a planet of good fortune. It represents our opportunities for success, prosperity, and abundance. It also represents our ability to attract good luck and positive outcomes.

Wisdom: Jupiter is a planet of wisdom. It represents our ability to learn and grow from our experiences. It also represents our ability to see the big picture and make wise decisions.

Justice: Jupiter is a planet of justice. It represents our sense of fairness and our desire to see that everyone is treated fairly. It also represents our ability to uphold the law and promote justice.

In a natal chart, Jupiter's placement can indicate:

Our areas of growth and expansion: Jupiter's placement can indicate the areas of our lives where we have the greatest potential for growth and expansion.

Our opportunities for good fortune: Jupiter's placement can indicate the areas of our lives where we have the greatest opportunities for success, prosperity, and abundance.

Our capacity for wisdom: Jupiter's placement can indicate our capacity for learning and growing from our experiences.

Our sense of justice: Jupiter's placement can indicate our sense of fairness and our desire to see that everyone is treated fairly.

Basic Concepts to Use in Elemental Interpretation:

Jovial

Kind

Theatrical

Lazy

Good-natured

Careless

Argumentative

Condescending

In General Interpretation:

Long journeys

Prosperous or satisfactory situations

Emanation of wealth and well-being

Relationships with justice, law, or law

Abstract manifestations

People or places that produce admiration

Excessive increases

Political relatives

The Deities that Emanate from the Influence of Jupiter:

The ancients must have perceived the magnitude of the planet Jupiter in its influence on living beings and placed this giant planet at the head of their altars.

In Assyro-Babylonian mythology, the planet Jupiter is known as Bel, which means lord. In Sumer, he was considered the master and lord of the atmospheric zone and had as attributes the storm, the lightning, and the flood.

These attributes, along with other representations, appear again in Greek and Hebrew mythology.

In all their legends, from Bel to Jehovah, Jupiter is the god of the flood, and he uses this alteration of the elements to modify the life of the earth. Jupiter is therefore a great modifier.

On the other hand, in all myths, he appears as the god who organizes the Universe, separates day from night; gives brightness to the Sun, the Moon, and the stars. He is a kind of universal arbiter whose wisdom and justice regulate all things. Everything came from him; good, evil, and even destiny.

As a god of the heavens, it was assumed that the place closest to him was found at the summits of mountains, properly representing the "most high".

For this reason, he was honored in the highest places, such as Mount Liceus, Olympus, Athos, or, in its translation to Judaism, on Mount Sinai.

Lightning is the weapon and the main attribute of Zeus' Piter, Jupiter, and symbolizes in its active form the celestial fire, the spark of life, and the fertilizing power.

The lightning is compared with his way of manifesting himself, *",...there came thunder and lightning and a thick cloud over the mountain, and loud noises very loud, ...the whole mountain of Sinai was smoking because Jehovah had come down "*(Ex. 19).

"Voice of Jehovah that pours out flames of fire" (Psalm 29). Similarly, Jupiter appears thundering, shaking the world with its overwhelming thunder.

In his different myths, Jupiter always appears as a multifaceted, promiscuous, and polygamous god; he not only united sexually with different divinities, but he also had sexual relations with humans and had offspring, whether divine, semi-divine, heroic, or prophetic. Because of having this offspring, he is given the symbolism of fatherhood, hence his name of Zeus-Piter, Jupiter.

The Greek Zeus, to maintain his reproductive relations with humans, adopted the most diverse transformations or metamorphoses, since his splendid presence killed Semele, mother of Dionysus. He transformed himself into a bull to have relations with Europa, from whose union Minos was born; he metamorphosed into a swan with Leda, from which Polydeuces and Helen were born; in the form of a golden shower to fertilize Danae, giving birth to Perseus, or imitating Amphitryon to beget Heracles, to cite the most famous or known transformations.

In the Hebrew myth of Jehovah, this intimate relationship of love and fatherhood or procreation with humans also appears; sometimes Jupiter appears directly as Jehovah and sometimes through his angels or transformations. (Gen 21) *"Jehovah visited Sarah, as he had said, and Jehovah did with Sarah as he had spoken, and Sarah conceived Isaac."*

Parallel to the Greek Zeus, Jehovah is also considered the father of the gods, heroes, and prophets. A clear case is with Samson, the Hercules of the Jews:

An angel of Jehovah appeared to Manoa and said to him (Judg 13) "Behold, you are barren, and you have never had children, but you will conceive and give birth to a son, and you will call him Samson."

Another angel said to Zechariah; (Luke 13) *"Do not be afraid, for your prayer has been heard, and your wife will bear you a son, and you will call him John."*

–The angel Gabriel was sent by God (Deus, Zeus) to a city of Galilee called Nazareth, to a virgin of the house of David named Mary. (Luke 1–28) *"And the angel entered where she was, and said, 'Hail, highly favored one!'"*

"The Lord is with you; blessed are you among women.....And now you will conceive in your womb,

and you will give birth to a son, and you will call his name Jesus. He will be great, and he will be called the Son of the Highest. . . "

With this last passage, the myth of the father god, Zeus-Piter, Jupiter, is repeated.

This interrelationship of Jupiter among humans is also evoked in shamanic cultures around the world. The legend of the Siberian shamans says *that "the Highest sent the eagle to the aid of humans; it impregnated a woman, and she gave birth to the first shaman."* Castaneda's Eagle would also be a representation of this mirror of the almighty divinity.

The color blue is the color of Krishna, one of the incarnations of Vishnu, the most charming and human of the incarnations. "Krishna bewitches all women by the pleasure he awakens in them."

Applied to an object, the color blue lightens the forms, opens them, and dissolves them. The sky blue is the path of dreaming, (Jupiter, ruler of the ninth house). Conscious thought gives way to the abstract mind, so it is related to abstract cultural manifestations or religious dramas.

In Buddhism, the color blue is the color of wisdom, potentiality, and simultaneously of emptiness. It therefore represents the focus of attention on religion, philosophy, and higher education.

In the legends, we saw how Jupiter always appears in the middle of a crash. Likewise, in its cyclical stagings of human life, it usually produces a "too much", with sensations of much, copious, or too much, it is therefore normal that it contributes to excesses of growth. (A notable increase in weight is detected in a very high percentage of people when Jupiter transits through the first house.)

It also makes its influence felt in exaggerated or disordered growth when associated with other planets, for example, in transits of Jupiter over Neptune in the sixth house, curable diseases are detected, due to disordered cellular growth.

Symbolism of Saturn

Saturn is the second largest planet in our solar system, after Jupiter. It is also the largest of the gas giants. Saturn is unique in appearance, with its iconic rings. The rings are made up of billions of small particles of ice, rock, and dust. They are not solid, but rather a collection of individual particles that orbit Saturn.

The rings of Saturn can be seen from Earth from different angles as the planet orbits the Sun. When the rings are seen edge-on, they are not visible. However, when the rings are seen face-on, they appear as a bright band around the planet.

Saturn has over 80 moons, but the largest is Titan. Titan is the only moon in the solar system with a thick atmosphere. It is also the only moon with lakes of liquid methane on its surface.

Saturn is the last planet visible to the naked eye, without the use of any artificial aid, so it has been known since antiquity as the limit of the solar system visible to the human eye. Therefore, it represents in astrology the limits of the material, all kinds of limits and limitations.

The astrological influence of the planet Saturn is staged, on a personal level, as the plane of consciousness that one has as a father, as a boss. Saturn influences through the paternalistic sense, which in its positive aspect has to do with affection and care, in contrast to the matriarchy associated with the Moon.

Saturn emits a "package of integrated data in differential quantum radio frequency" that makes us prone to saving and conservation, to some more and others less. Saturn stages its influence in the attitudes of moderation and prudence, but that same moderating influence can lead to meanness, greed for fear of scarcity, cold, or hunger.

The scenes that are typical of the influence of Saturn are situations of restriction, when what is needed is scarce and can be felt as hunger, cold, or discomfort and tightness, it is also staged in unpleasant events. In this negative aspect, Saturn is associated with the feeling of bad luck; to misfortune, as the ancients called it, unhappiness, need, and misery, and it is related to the feeling of abandonment, pessimism, austerity, and parsimony, this last as a reflection of the slowness of the planet.

Generally, the influence of Saturn is perceived as heaviness and control. It is noticeable in restrictive situations that require waiting, in temporal impediments and material conditioning, such as waiting, delays, and postponements of all kinds.

A perfect example of the influence of Saturn is what is staged when we have to go through airport security, a place associated with Aquarius, a sign that has been ruled by Saturn since antiquity. Saturn is the security control, and Uranus is the airplanes.

At the individual level, the influence of Saturn is present when we act responsibly. It is the principle of fulfilling responsibilities and corresponds to the awareness of material security.

It can also be associated with the feeling of security that erudite knowledge produces. It represents the wisdom that is enclosed in encyclopedias, and it has to do with concrete and practical cultural manifestations.

Saturn is associated with that which implies duration of time. It represents stability and the strength of the material. On a personal level, it manifests itself in the moral strength that makes one remain constant in the pursuit of what has been begun. It corresponds to the state of what does not move or waver. It is the permanent duration of an attitude, associated with all kinds of crystallizations and the perpetuation of the established.

When the influence of Saturn cannot or does not know how to be channeled, it does so through the father or any person who has authority over one, such as a boss or a superior. If there is no father, boss, or superior, Saturn is channeled through erudite study and a controlled and measured life, or control over diet and lifestyle, controlling schedules or attitudes.

If one is not a father, nor does one have a boss, nor does one give an outlet to the energy of the constant beating of the planet Saturn, nor does one exercise any control over one's diet, nor over one's vital schedules, and one lives without control, then its influence is diverted towards the material part, being able to affect the spleen in some people, the organ of joy, which when it is affected, joy is lost. It can also be diverted towards the bones, especially the joints, knees, shoulders, and elbows, and especially teeth and molars. Although there are a few other people who are directly affected by the right ear, leaving this ear more deaf than the left.

Types of Joints

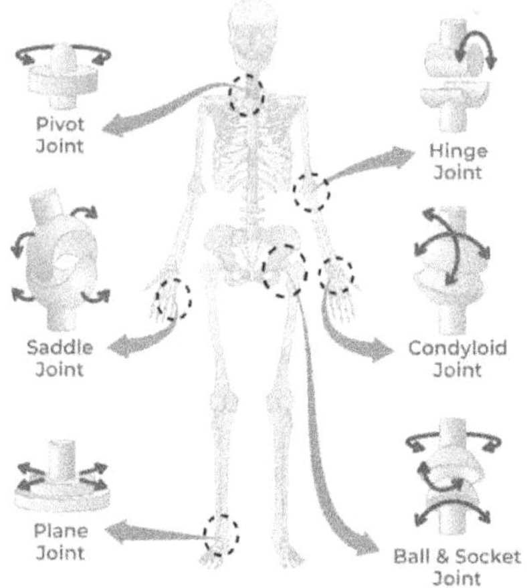

Keywords and General Concepts of Saturn

Economical

Cautious

Discreet

Fulfilling

Shy

Pessimistic

Rigid

Protective

Restrictive situations and hardships

Concrete cultural manifestations

Fulfillment of responsibilities

Impediments or material conditioning

Unpleasant or unpleasant events

Crystallization of all kinds

Father, boss; immediate superior authority

Old age and land seizures

The Deities that Emanate from the Astrological Influence of Saturn

In Orphic cosmogony, Cronus, the Greek name for Saturn, ruled the universe alongside Rhea, the Earth, also known as Isis.

Saturn fulfilled his promise to swallow all his male children, wanting to represent in this way the function of time, which gives rise and end to species in the life of our planet regulates the natural cycles of species, and prevents the special predominance of one species over the others. Thus, the predominance of the large reptiles was swallowed by time.

For the Orphics, the reign of Saturn or of time encompasses the space before the appearance of Jupiter and with it, the appearance of humanity, when a multitude of animal and plant species appear that have systematically been swallowed by time, eliminated by the evolution of species.

Perhaps for this reason, the Romans represented Saturn as an ancient nature divinity and associated him with an agricultural god. His name Saturn can be related to "satur", which means, saturated, satiated, fed up, and is synonymous with something that swallows everything.

In ancient representations it appeared with the figure of a vigorous old man, covered in red garments, with white hair and beard, carrying as attributes an hourglass in one hand and a scythe in the other.

The scythe appears as a symbol of death only in the 15th century, but in previous traditions, it is a symbol of harvest, abundance, and food.

In the Greek legend of Cronus, he uses the scythe to amputate part of the reproductive organ of his father Uranus, but does not produce any death with this utensil.

The scythe is the attribute of several agricultural deities and is related to food and harvesting. The scythe is used to reap cereals, so it represents the beginning of productive technology, so Saturn is associated with the beginning of the production of food on a massive scale.

The hourglass symbolizes the perpetual fall of time, its inexorable flow, and the consummation of the cycles of life; but it also represents the possibility of time reversal, it is the symbol of the inversion of relationships between the upper and lower world.

In another sense, the hourglass represents the small and continuous dripping of the grains that will be lost in the transfer of wild cereal to the village, thus producing the progressive emigration of cereals towards the proximity of human habitat.

The attributes of Saturn speak to us of gathering agriculture, food supply, and animal domestication. Today, its influence has established its kingdom on Earth in large shopping centers.

The model of Saturnian divinity does not correspond, as one might think, to an isolated and dark deity representing the immobility of time. Saturn is like the other planetary gods, a living and immortal god that survives as always in the substrate of humans and is present in the collective unconscious of humanity.

(In reality, someone has to say it, we are the substrate or the humus that serves to give life to the planetary gods, the food of the archangels, as Gurdjieff very well defined.)

The presence and influence of the Saturnian deity is so intense, and its power is so strong, that it is one of the gods that receives one of the most important cults.

In the Western world, where the luminous aspect of the deity of Saturn is more deeply rooted, festivals have been celebrated in his honor since the most ancient times, going back to the times when, after all the harvesting had been done, it was necessary to consume all the perishable foods. In these times, there was eating to satiety, swallowing, devouring, it was the feast of the satiator, and it was appropriate to retain a maximum of reserves in the organism in order to be able to cross the harsh winter that announces its presence.

Today, as in any previous era, the same celebration is still held in his honor. Every year, with the entry of the Sun into Capricorn – the domicile of Saturn – the model of this celestial divinity appears throughout the orb of Western culture; thousands of representations of the new Saturn can be seen, only that, based on so much feasting, the model of Saturn has gained weight and has changed its name to disguise it.

Now Saturn stages its presence in human form, just like in ancient Greece, as a vigorous old man, covered in red garments, with white hair and beard, like the Greek model, but now he is quite a bit fatter and rosier, the "time" has suited him well.

The attributes have also changed, now he rides in a sleigh pulled by reindeer and is known as Santa Claus.

This luminous model, in one of its aspects, like the ancestral model, represents consumerism, it is the pattern of our capitalist society.

But this is only the representation of Saturn related to the luminous aspect of the planet, it is the celestial father who rewards with goods and offers gifts to those who have fulfilled their responsibilities, and who punishes with black coal those who have failed to meet their obligations.

Every manifestation is dual. Saturn, like the other planets, also has a negative, magnetic, centripetal, dark, and absorbent side. The planets are the gods, the angels, and also the demons. The dark side of Saturn has a direct relationship with the satanic and with Satan himself.

That is why Saturn also stages the dark side of the divine, the gravitational force of matter, which in one of its manifestations is perfectly represented by the black stone of the Kaaba, the axis of a patriarchal and paternalistic religion before the Prophet, in which its followers still revolve around the black stone, emulating the neither solid nor liquid rings of the planet to which they are subject; it is no coincidence that Capricorn has always been assigned to Arab culture and religion in contrast to Jupiter, which is Judeo-Christian. It is also no coincidence that they built the world's largest and heaviest clock in Mecca.

Symbolism of Uranus

Uranus is the seventh planet in our solar system. The first of the new trans-Neptunians. It is considered a planet with special characteristics. Its way of rotating is completely different from the rest of the planets; while the other planets rotate without hardly varying their axis concerning the ecliptic plane, Uranus tilts its axis up to 98º, giving the image that it is rolling down a circular corridor.

The name Uranus was given to it by the astronomer Johan Bode, its theoretical discoverer along with Daniel Titus, who proposed the law now known as Titus-Bode or Bode's law. These laws allow us to predict the existence of a new planet in the place where Herchel observed what he believed to be a comet.

Similar to Saturn, Uranus also has rings, but they are much smaller and less bright. So far, nine very narrow rings are known – seven of them less than 100 kilometers wide. These rings are very dark and between them, there are numerous shepherd moons, apart from its five known satellites.

Uranus is the first planet, to be observed by human beings, some artifice must be used because it cannot be seen by the eye naturally. Its observation requires some technique.

The first symbolic analogy that we can draw from these special characteristics is its correspondence with the principle of the immaterial. That is why Uranus is staged through the techniques that promote evolutionary situations and new ways of seeing things, it is similar to the cosmic force that forces new revisions and provokes unpredictable changes; unlike the periodic and predictable lunar changes. Uranus always comes on stage with sudden and unexpected changes, unthinkable differences, the new and the unknown.

After the discovery of Uranus, new perspectives opened up for celestial observation. From the discovery of Uranus, a new dark system begins, invisible but real. By similarity, Uranus is perceived in an immaterial way, invisible, but actively, as electricity is perceived, to which it is associated.

For some people, electricity can feel like something great and very useful, while for others, who do not use any devices, it can be an unpleasant surprise.

The first time we "experience" electricity is usually when we get a shock from the current or see a lightning bolt. Then we feel that bright and trembling emergence that provokes awe, and respect, and leaves us with a moved spirit. Everyone finds out what electricity is after receiving a shock and a good scare.

This is how Uranus is staged.

Because it is higher than Saturn, Uranus is associated with things that can fly above the Earth, such as airplanes, but not balloons, which are Neptunian. It has been shown that the Jupiter-Uranus cycles are closely related to the progress of aeronautics and astronautics.

Uranus influences in the same way as the other planets, and when it flows through a person, it can be staged with the exclamation of "Eureka!" or "I did it!" Uranus comes on stage with that cry of victory that is exclaimed when a brilliant idea has been perceived. – The more Uranian a person is, the more that scene is perceived.

Any manifestation of the influence of Uranus can be considered surprising or unexpected; it is always related to unforeseen or unpredictable events.

In its astrological application, we can say that it is related to everything that has innovative, special, or different characteristics from what is already known; we can also associate it with what is not of natural origin, but rather devised or invented.

In astrological interpretation, we will associate it with all sudden transformations and evolutions of all kinds, with unforeseen changes that move, such as revolts, disorders, imbalances, and collective and tumultuous events that produce fear or respect.

Uranus represents mutation, inversion, crisis, novelty, alteration, and innovation. At the individual level, when its influence possesses us, it can be perceived in acts of going from one extreme to the other, taking another turn, being another person, or changing a milestone. In politics, Uranus, because it has its domicile in Aquarius, the sign opposite to Leo, the sign of royalty, is staged in all republican movements.

Most of its stagings are usually related to disorder, confusion, anomalies, irregularities, and disagreements that generally lead to division, disunity, disengagement, separation, or independence. Therefore, Uranus has a direct influence on all types of separatist or independence politics.

In astrology, Uranus is associated with a level of consciousness similar to that of Mercury, that is, of a mental type, but more intense and more vast. Uranus is the consciousness that transcends the temporal, crosses the boundaries of time, and allows us to conceive things in an atemporal way, representing the possibility of perceiving what has not yet happened, the vision of the future. – Julio Verne is a magnificent representative of this type of Uranian consciousness.--

Uranus is also related to the first awareness of the collective and the need to seek one's individuality. Uranus is the need for self-knowledge, it is the form of knowledge that is achieved through a discipline such as psychoanalysis or astrology, to give two examples, but they are by no means the only ways.

In addition, the influence of Uranus is intimately linked to the manifestations of psi-gamma phenomena, or knowledge, and is directly related to intuition, – the lightning knowledge–

Finally, as a planet related to Aquarius and the eleventh house, it is associated with the characteristics of the "friend," and of group travel.

Age of Uranus

At the age of 82, the complete cycle of Uranus – which is formed at that age – closes the first cycle of this planet that demands evolution and change. This point marks a kind of border. A whole life of growth and change has helped me to become the unique individual that I am now. In that time, if one is still alive, many periods will have been experienced in which existence has been exciting and open. Even if any of them lived negatively, the final result was to know freedom and evolve. In this period of life, one possesses a freedom of perspective and evolved perceptions about life, which only age and experience can bring. This stage of life confers the highest degree of wisdom and serves to enter the next evolutionary stage.

In the human body, it is related to the electrical impulses that travel through the nervous system, the alterations of neurotransmitters, and the development of neurological diseases.

Uranus Words and Keywords

Character Destiny

ORIGINAL Separations, disunions

NONCONFORMIST Friends and group travel

INDEPENDENT Unforeseen events

DISRESPECTFUL Sudden transformations, evolutions

SACRIFICED Original and unexpected events

UTOPIAN Tumultuous collective events

REBEL Tense or explosive situations

INVENTIVE Disorders, disagreements

Objects and Places

Internet, the Web

Electrical Objects

Appliances

Telephone

Airplanes

Computer

Electric Blanket

Electric Chair

Additional Notes

A Female Model of Uranus: Athena

Classical mythology is not very helpful in understanding the female model of Uranus, as the planet was named after the Greek god Uranus, who was the father of the Titans.

Some astrologers believe that Uranus can be interpreted as the higher octave of Mercury, while others describe it as electrical and violent. In a syncretic approach, one could say that the most typical model would be represented by an archetype that is intermediate between Mars and Mercury.

Due to the lack of luminosity of the planet, it would be necessary to add dark traits or gravitational forces, that is, feminine. In this way, the model of Palas Athena fits perfectly. The majority of current astrologers have perfectly integrated this archetype.

Minerva, the Latin name of Palas Athena, has several legends about her birth. The last known one tells that her father was the giant Palas (son of the Earth) who tried to rape her, because of this, the goddess killed him, skinned him, and with his skin made the aegis (a breastplate of virginity). To seal her victory she assumed the warlike name of Palas Athena.

In another legend, she is associated with Poseidon (Neptune), perhaps because of her proximity to the zodiac sign; Uranus or Minerva rules the sign of Aquarius and Neptune the neighboring sign of Pisces. On the other hand, Neptune is the divinity that dominates the liquid element of the seas, while Minerva, born on the banks of a lake, symbolizes the lightning that precedes the rains; Aquarius precedes Pisces.

But the most famous legend considers her the daughter of Zeus and Metis (wisdom). It is said that Metis was Zeus' first lover. While Metis was pregnant, Gea and Uranus told Zeus that after giving him a daughter, Metis would give him a son who would depose him, just as he had deposed Cronos. Then Zeus swallowed Metis, who was already carrying Athena in her womb. Shortly thereafter, Zeus felt severe headaches, so severe that they became so unbearable that he asked Hephaestus to relieve them in any way possible. Hephaestus, according to some, or Prometheus, according to others, opened his skull with his bronze sword. Through the open wound and giving a prolonged cry of victory, Athena emerged; "clad in shining armor and wielding a steel javelin". Seeing her, a feeling of respect and awe gripped all the immortals. "The vast Olympus was shaken by the impetuous emergence of the goddess with the radiant eyes."

The most famous representation is the Athena of the Parthenon, a work by Phidias. She is covered in a long tunic, wears a helmet on her head, and her chest, the aegis, her right arm rests on the javelin or spear, and her right-hand holds a winged victory.

From these attributes, we can extract a practical symbolism. The tunic that covers her body marks a notable difference from the other divinities that generally go uncovered, this concealment of the body possibly symbolizes the impossibility of seeing the planet with the naked eye, with which it is associated.

The spear is a male symbol and indicates strength and authority. In legal activities, it represented the protection of contracts, processes, and debates.

The aegis, at first, symbolized the storm that generates terror and panic, but unlike the lightning bolt, it is not a weapon intended to strike, but rather a psychological weapon that seeks to inspire fear and incite mortals not to put their trust in anyone but those who deserve it, as Chevalier relates.

The helmet is a symbol of invisibility, invulnerability, and power. The helmet of Athena, like that of Pluto, made whoever wore it invisible, the helmet protects by making it invisible. When Athena came to the aid of Diomedes to fight Ares, she wore the helmet that characterized her.

Athena is a chaste goddess, she never lets herself be carried away by her amorous impulse, which contrasts curiously with the rest of the inhabitants of Olympus. Despite the slanderous insinuations about her supposed relationships with Helios, Hephaestus, and Hercules; one day while she was bathing, she was surprised by Tiresias (a famous Greek astrologer, created by Homer, who was blinded for having seen Athena naked. Lucian believed that it was because he had assured that the planets had two sexes) and although the indiscretion was involuntary, she punished him by depriving him of his sight.

This brutal act denotes a degree of cruelty in the archetype, typical of Aquarians, creating a contradiction between compassion for the strong, in favor of whom she mobilized all her potential.

Finally, this divinity has a warlike and warrior character, surpassing even the god of war. Although she only used it to help the heroes worthy of her compassion.

Her birth symbolizes a luminous and shaking emergence – like lightning –, which provokes amazement, produces respect, and moves the spirit. – Athena comes out of the head –, it is related to what is not tangible in a natural way, but remarkable.

The female model of Aquarius is undoubtedly the goddess of the shining eyes. Her influence on women is such that almost all of them can be recognized by those large or lively eyes with which they look at you as if they were a magnifying glass that undresses you.

In Greek mythology, it is narrated that the other gods were taken aback, for they say that upon seeing her, a feeling of respect and amazement overwhelmed all the immortals. Therefore, the woman Athena must have characteristics that inspire respect and surprise. Generally, those large eyes stand out, which come close to the image of the goddess of the shining eyes. The Athena woman stands out for her eyes, her gaze that seems to penetrate everything, her way of looking big and open that makes us feel that she discovers everything we carry inside.

Indeed, Athena is a very enigmatic model. The ideal or pure female model is the chaste or unvoluptuous woman who never gave in to her love impulse or who feels male sexuality as aggression. This anomaly must have an explanation, since in her different myths, several situations appear in which someone tries to rape her. This could be associated with a model of a woman who has suffered an attempted rape or sexual assault and who has developed a protective shell to defend herself from such eventualities.

The fact of being born out of Zeus's head places her as the Goddess of Intelligence, but she was also a warrior goddess and, as Juan B. Bergua recounts, a Hippia, that is, a horse tamer. In reality, Athena teaches men to domesticate nature using ingenuity and shows them how to use the bridle of horses, although her favorite animal is the owl.

Athena is the protective divinity of acropolises and the guardian of cities. She inhabited the heights that had strategic importance. Athena presided over all the arts and works of peace. She was also known by the epithet *Ergane*, "the industrious worker." There was a proverb in the weaving workshops of Athens that said "to move one's fingers with the help of Athena," which indicated her mastery in all works.

She was also the patron of potters, for she, along with Hephaestus, was the one who modeled Pandora, the first figure of a woman, whom she left provided with the resources necessary to seduce men. But she was above all the goddess of reason and wisdom, for this reason, she personifies the reflective thought that both men and women influenced by Uranus enjoy.

When the Uranus model expresses itself from the feminine world, it does so through the woman Athena, a woman who faces life with a psychological weapon that seeks to inspire respect and surprise, qualities that allow her to incite others.

Athena is decidedly inciting and strategic. She usually does not act, or if she does, she does so by deploying her strategy, like generals or from a high or invisible place. Athena moves or stimulates others to do things, but she stays on the sidelines, she plays dumb.

The Athena personality has combative traits. She does not shy away from contradicting and confronting those who disagree with her. She may even take pleasure in her defensive actions, which denotes a degree of cruelty as in the archetype. They are always women in whom an authoritarian disposition and a strong character are appreciated, enough to fight or compete with men for any social or professional position. Their weapons are strategy, ingenuity, and their secret resources to seduce others.

In her book "The Goddesses," Manuela Dunn presents a model of Athena that is worth knowing:

"Women who have affinities with the archetype of Athena could be, for example, successful investors who can instinctively detect market movements and act accordingly, planning the timing and strategy. They can also be brilliant professionals, capable of discerning the intricacies of corporate politics and internal competition.

The woman Athena possesses the gift of feminine logical thinking, which is intuitive. She can keep her mind clear amid powerful emotions and provide practical solutions to complex problems. The woman Athena is an impartial judge, as the myth says; she can be an excellent professional advisor or business consultant, providing companies with carefully crafted management programs.

Always flanked by powerful heroes and gods, Athena can seem "masculine" and also very mature.

She undoubtedly possesses a moral and psychological integrity that is very different from that of any other goddess. Her wisdom is practical, her tactics cold and resolute. Her gift of strategy implies that she is aware of ethics and diplomacy; thus, she knows power and respects it. As a result, a woman Athena can be misunderstood by other women, as she is not considered "feminine" enough.

Powerful men often trust women with the qualities of Athena and seek her advice. In her later years, the woman Athena may well be almost a magician, a strategist of destiny who advises others how to advance in their projects towards the achievement of an intense and satisfying life."

The Goddess of Aquarius will be the new model for humanity to imitate. The Piscean Age is ending, and the crucified Christ model is clearly in decline. Meanwhile, the influence of women is becoming increasingly noticeable, especially in the Western world, where everything has changed for years and they already enjoy an equality never before imagined.

The values of the Goddess will be the values of the new religion, of the new way of facing the phenomenon of divinity. The Goddess is coming. Who will be her representatives? Who will be her priestesses?

Symbolism of Neptune

Neptune is the eighth planet in our solar system. It is a gas giant and is the farthest planet from the Sun. It is so far away that it cannot be seen with the naked eye. It was discovered in 1846 by Urbain Le Verrier, who used mathematics to predict its existence based on the perturbations it was causing in the orbit of Uranus.

The symbol for Neptune is a stylized trident, the weapon of the Roman god Neptune. The trident represents Neptune's power over the sea and the underworld. It also represents the planet's association with dreams, illusions, and spirituality.

Neptune is the planet of dreams, illusions, and spirituality. It is associated with the unconscious mind, intuition, and creativity. It is also associated with the sea, water, and the underworld.

The two moons of Neptune, Triton and Nereid, are also associated with the planet's symbolism. Triton is a large, icy moon with a very eccentric orbit. It is named after the son of Neptune. Nereid is a small, irregular moon with a very eccentric orbit. It is named after the wife of Neptune.

The symbolism of Neptune is complex and multifaceted. It is a planet that represents the hidden, mysterious, and spiritual aspects of life.

These moons, instead of rotating in the equatorial plane of the central body and the same direction of rotation, as occurs in other systems, have an anomalous rotation; the orbits of these satellites are very inclined concerning the equator. Triton's orbit is retrograde, while Nereid forms a very elongated ellipse.– The eccentricity that we previously appreciated in Uranus, when we talk about Neptune, is transferred to the moons.

The two known moons of Neptune, Triton and Nereid (son and wife of this mythological god), are notably eccentric. As are these two characters in the myth, half human and half fish.

In the case of Neptune, the nomination seems very accurate, which will allow us to know with some ease its symbolic message.

These moons, instead of rotating in the equatorial plane of the central body and the same direction of rotation, as occurs in other systems, have an anomalous rotation; the orbits of these satellites are very inclined concerning the equator. Triton's orbit is retrograde, while Nereid forms a very elongated ellipse.– The eccentricity that we previously appreciated in Uranus, when we talk about Neptune, is transferred to the moons.

In the case of Neptune, the nomination seems very accurate, which will allow us to know with some ease its symbolic message.

Similar to its system of moons, the events or relationships associated with the influence of

Neptune in the astrological field, are often staged in situations related to people who tend to group in an eccentric or anomalous way the beings that fall within their sphere of action; as is the case with religious leaders, sects, or idealistic political groups.

In the ancient myth, Neptune is the conspirator. In the division of the world, Neptune was given the sovereignty of the seas. (the world of feelings). Neptune accepted it for lack of anything better, resigned but not satisfied. Thus was born in him the idea of conspiring against Jupiter.

One of the special characteristics of Neptune can be seen in acts of proselytism or the desire for expansion. In the myth, it is said that: *"Neptune's thirst for domination was proverbial, to the point that it often caused conflicts with the other gods".*

The influence of Neptune is staged in a magnetic, dominant, and enveloping way. In the legend, he had famous disputes. To assert his right over Attica, he struck the rock of the Acropolis with his trident and a fountain of salt water sprang from it. Because of this, he had to face Athena, the protector of Athens. The gods settled the dispute in favor of Athena. Thus, a lawsuit between knowledge (Athena-Uranus) and imagination (Neptune) was left open, which persists today.

He also disputed with Hera the possession of Argolis, and he ran with the same luck, the verdict was unfavorable to him. He sued Helios for the possession of the Isthmus of Corinth; in this case, Briareus, a son of Uranus, was the one who ruled to cede Acrocorintus to Helios, leaving the rest of the isthmus for Poseidon. He also disputed with Zeus the possession of Aegina and with Apollo the territory of Delphi, without any success.

The undisputed kingdom of Neptune is the sea; the free waters without borders.

"The sea symbolizes a transitional state between the still informal possibilities and the formal realities, a situation of ambiguity that is that of

uncertainty, doubt, indecision, and that can end well or badly" (Chevalier).

The sea is made up of waters, *"the waters, undifferentiated mass, represent the infinity of the possible."* Water is also a symbol of spiritual life. The captivity and uncertainty of the nights of Saint John of the Cross and his Spiritual Canticle are possibly the highest note of consciousness that this planet can bestow.

Being one of the slowest planets – it takes about fourteen years to cross each of the different zodiac signs – it exerts a generational or collective influence. It is therefore related to all human groupings of an ideal or abstract nature.

From its sphere of activity, generally magnetic, the induction arises to join others for some ideal, invisible, unreal, or utopian purpose. From singing in a choir to being part of a community dedicated to spiritual meditation by some master of the time. Whenever Neptune manifests itself on the collective plane, it reflects the anomalies of its moons, creating eccentricities or retrogradations that lead collectives to unreal, retrograde, or involutionary situations.

Neptune is comparable to involutions or all attempts of this nature, such as the acts of February 24 in Spain or those of August 1991 in Russia. This aspect of Neptune is presented as the greatest obstacle to the evolution of human beings, either through its reflections in politics or religion, both associated with Neptune.

Neptune is identified as something that covers or hides in a veiled way; like frosted glass in bathrooms, veils, or curtains; mists of all kinds, natural or artificial. It is the music and smoke of the botafumeiro in churches and also the colored smoke of the Rokc shows of today. −Rock is not understood without taking anything−

Neptune is always related to what envelops coldly and is irresistibly attractive. Neptune is the whole world of drugs and medications. In certain people, the lack of this bewitching influence is known as "withdrawal syndrome".

In everyday life, we can associate Neptune with idealistic or mysterious experiences that attract attention and that do not make logical sense.

Neptune is vibrant in hidden or reserved events, its sphere of action is usually shrouded in dark and strange situations, but it is never anything evident. The influence of Neptune is present in all moments where people gather and amazement is produced with delight, such as in concerts or masses.

Neptune comes to the scene in illusions, fantasies, and fables; these are the myths and legends that are inserted in our deep unconscious, linked to certain groups of humanity.

As the ruler of Pisces and the twelfth house, it is attributed to illness and dirt. –Ernesto Cordero goes so far as to affirm that Neptune are the spots; that which in personal life, dirties or spoils a parcel of existence

Of course, Neptune also has positive or luminous aspects, that is, activators of group consciousness. Its influence facilitates the perception of collective consciousness and allows us to participate and enjoy in a collective way, such as singing in a choir or participating in a religious ceremony.

When one is under the radiant influence of this planet, one can perceive all of humanity as a single being linked to the divine or ideal. In that state of consciousness, one is all with One. This is the wonderful experience that the luminous aspect of Neptune grants. But to perceive this fine and subtle influence of Neptune, on a personal level, it is almost essential to resort to some artifice, skill, training, or have a special conformation; privilege of a few.

Neptune can be perceived or appreciated as good music, in the presence of works of art, or savoring wine. Neptune is the subtle and special note of distinction, which allows us to taste certain delights of a superior or higher quality. In a sense, it is comparable to the bubbles in champagne.

Neptune operates in all states of altered consciousness caused by the ingestion of any type of substance. It is also the green of the crosses on pharmacies and everything that exists behind them. Neptune is analogous to mixing, emulsifying, dissolving, filtering, macerating, and infusing.

The sphere of individual activity of Neptune is confined to the deep unconscious, where it is necessary to dive to know or appreciate its effects; which are always of a psychic nature.

It is also related to that strange influence that can grant to the human being, the gift of knowing by inspiration, distant or future things, as well as a singularity in artistic creativity.

Neptune represents the state of consciousness that is the key that opens the door to the Muses. It is also associated with the possibility of seeing in mental images real or ideal things; Neptune is the imagination, with all its action potential.

In other words, Neptune is associated with the realm of the subconscious mind. It is the realm of dreams, intuition, and spirituality. Neptune can give us insights into the deeper meaning of life, and it can inspire us to create beautiful and meaningful art.

Here are some specific examples of how Neptune can manifest in our lives:

Intuition: Neptune can give us a gut feeling about something, even if we don't have any logical reason to believe it. This intuition can be very helpful in making decisions, or in avoiding danger.

Creativity: Neptune is the planet of creativity. It can inspire us to create art, music, literature, or anything else that expresses our inner vision.

Spirituality: Neptune is associated with spirituality and mysticism. It can help us to connect with a higher power, or to experience a sense of oneness with the universe.

Neptune in its negative aspect, is comparable to the experience of separation from the other beings that surround us, which makes us feel different because of something that is carried as marked, "ingested" or infected, whether by an illness or by a collective idea. Neptune is always represented as an altered, artificial, or acquired state of consciousness. It is related to collective idealism. Drug dependencies are imposed on personal will, and altered thoughts, produced by the intake of certain drugs or the performance of certain dramas.

Its negative side is always incomprehensible and is associated with fanaticism and the dogmas of faith. Neptune demands trusting an assumption, of a group that usually encloses or hides an enigmatic individual, a pretender, a simulator, an impostor, or a false character.

As in a dream, Neptune represents all unconscious manifestations, the illusions of the senses or the mirages of the soul. It always manifests itself in alterations of reality and disorders of consciousness.

The worst manifestation of Neptune can be translated into disappointments, setbacks, scams, infidelities, and lies. It represents situations in which hope is lost for an ideal or a person. Neptune in its negative aspect is disappointment, deception, and disillusionment.

Its esoteric symbolism also has two aspects; one positive, creative, and full of life, which always manifests itself individually and allows us to reach higher states of consciousness; as in clairvoyance or ecstasy, and another negative and destructive that is always perceived as a collective level, interrupting personal impulses of will; as in moments of collective hysteria or the hallucinations of certain groups of individuals, some see the Virgin and others see extraterrestrials.

For those who are more esoterically informed, it must be said that the *"Tree of Life"* is related to Daath, the Shefira of the Abyss, or the Shefira hid behind the clouds of the Sanctuary. Neptune represents the intermediate point between

Understanding and Wisdom (Chokman and Binah). The name Daath brings the idea of realization in consciousness. It is the last stage before completion.**

In other words, the negative aspect of Neptune can lead to:

Disappointment: Neptune can lead to disappointment, as we find that our expectations are not met. This can lead to feelings of sadness, anger, and frustration.

Deception: Neptune can lead to deception, as we are misled or lied to. This can lead to feelings of betrayal, anger, and resentment.

Disillusionment: Neptune can lead to disillusionment, as we lose faith in something or someone. This can lead to feelings of sadness, anger, and despair.

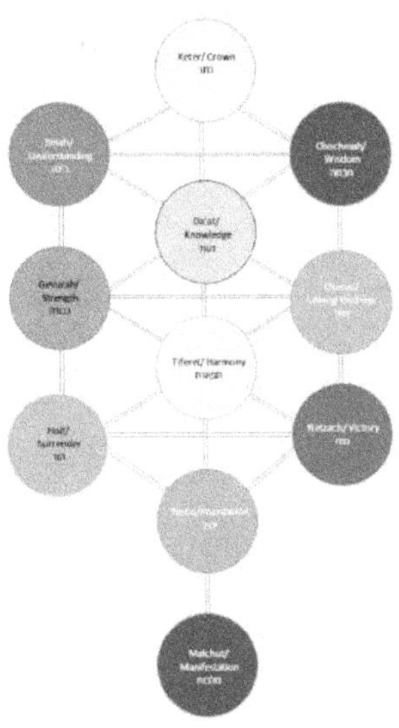

If Uranus represented the level of consciousness of the astrologer or psychologist, Neptune is the living symbol that is always transforming. Therefore, it is associated with the politician, who has come to fill the void left by the cleric.

At another point in time, it could symbolize the clergy, but today it can be associated with politicians of a socialist tendency and all ideologies that imply that the rights of each individual are derived from the collectivity and attribute to the State the power to order the conditions of civil, economic and political life, accentuating the preponderance of the collective interest over that of the individual.

In other words, the author is arguing that Neptune is the planet of transformation and collectivism. It is associated with the politician because the politician is responsible for shaping the future of society. In the past, the cleric was responsible for this task, but in modern times, the politician has taken on this role.

Neptune, like a good politician, acts in a way of concealment, with a high degree of dissimulation, with maximum discretion, with reservations, and secrecy. Neptune is also associated with sanctimoniousness, bigotry, crocodile tears, simulation, and second intention.

The reason for associating Neptune with the topic of religiosity comes from its direct relationship with diseases. The human species, in general, only remembers God when it is sick. It is then that those crocodile tears come out saying; My God, my God, save me.

Neptune has a lot to do with the disordered cellular development that occurs due to deep emotional alterations that, as Dr. Haner says; are the origin of the development of many cancer diseases.**

In other words, the author is arguing that Neptune is associated with concealment, deception, and hypocrisy. This is because Neptune is the planet of illusion and fantasy. It can lead us to believe things that are not true or to act in ways that are not in our best interests.

The author also points out that Neptune is associated with religiosity. This is because Neptune is associated with deep emotional states. When we are sick, we are often in a state of great emotional distress. This can lead us to turn to religion for comfort and support.

Finally, the author argues that Neptune is associated with cancer. This is because Neptune is associated with disordered cellular development. When we are under a lot of stress, our cells can become damaged. This damage can lead to cancer.

Here are some specific examples of how Neptune can manifest in the context of politics, religion, and health:

Politics: Neptune can be used to manipulate people and deceive them. For example, a politician might use Neptune to create a false sense of hope or to distract people from their real problems.

Religion: Neptune can be used to exploit people's emotions. For example, a religious leader might use Neptune to make people feel guilty or to convince them to give their money or time.

Health: Neptune can be associated with chronic illnesses or illnesses that are difficult to diagnose or treat. For example, cancer is often associated with Neptune.

Neptune Keywords

Character:

Inspired: Unconscious manifestations, fantasies

Secretive: Idealistic or mysterious experiences

Apathetic: Hidden or reserved events

Fantastic: Dark or strange situations

Impressionable: Diseases

Confused: Disorders of consciousness

Selfless: Lies, deception, infidelity

Symbiotic: Idealistic groups or societies

Destiny:

Spirituality: Mysticism, religion

Creativity: Art, music, literature

Healing: Medicine, Psychology

Illusion: Deception, fantasy

Ecstasy: Spiritual enlightenment

Transcendence: Connection to a higher power

The keywords for Neptune are associated with its role as the planet of illusion, spirituality, and creativity. Neptune is associated with the subconscious mind, dreams, and intuition. It can also lead to deception, addiction, and escapism.

The character keywords for Neptune describe the way that Neptune can manifest in our personalities. Neptune-influenced people are often idealistic, imaginative, and spiritual. They can also be secretive, impressionable, and susceptible to deception.

The destiny keywords for Neptune describe the areas of life that are likely to be influenced by Neptune. Neptune-influenced people are often drawn to spirituality, creativity, and healing. They may also be prone to illusions, ecstasy, and transcendence.

Objects and Places

Pharmacies, drugs, and alcohol

Fats and oils

Musical objects

Cinemas, auditoriums, and theaters

Humid places

Dirty places

Remote places

Hospitals and hotels

Symbolism of Pluto

In the far reaches of our planetary system lies the smallest, but densest of the known planets. Pluto's density is still a matter of debate in astrophysical circles, but it is thought to be much higher than that of the rest of the planets.

It is true that for the "scientific authorities" Pluto is no longer a planet but a "dwarf planet". For us astrologers, it remains a needle in the great clock that is formed with our planetary system, a needle that tells the time and makes its influence felt in its time.

Like the other planets, astrologers resort to symbolism and analogies to extract maximum information about the type of astrological influence of the planet, its probable effects, as well as the archetype or representative model of the planet.

The reddish color that emanates from its spectral band directly associates it with the energies that we already know from the planet Mars – of whom it is thought to be the higher octave.

Pluto is the planet that takes the longest time to complete a full orbit. This slowness, combined with the eccentricity of its apparent passage through the zodiac signs (it was in Cancer for 26 years and only 11 in Libra and takes approximately 174 years to complete its cycle) connects it with major environmental changes or transformations and with the biological ages of ecosystems.

Pluto is the highest planet in the solar system, there is no other planet above it, so the level of consciousness related to Pluto elevates the human being above his species and allows us to experience an identification with the rest of nature, with the rest of the living beings.

The experience of Pluto breaks down the barriers of the ego, even going beyond the collective ego, beyond religious, socialist, or sectarian idealisms. With Pluto, ecological awareness appears in the most transcendental and pure sense. Therefore, Pluto is associated with Ecology and ecologists.

–At the end of times, probably, power will be shared between these and the plutocrats, the ecologists, and the "much richer", two sides of the same Pluto coin.

The manifestations of Pluto are perceived in the formation of what has come to be called "creative niches," tremendously active ecosystems where the highest survival values are found due to the intense grouping of individuals, such as the Rotary Club.

Intensity is qualitative and not quantitative, as was the case with the effects of Neptune.

The mythical and real invisibility of Pluto leads us to associate it with emptiness and everything whose special function is to have a space, such as caves, caverns, grottoes, underground spaces, shelters of any type, subways, etc.

Its influence is also perceived in crypts, niches, cemeteries, catacombs, and crematoria.

From the physical characteristics of the planet, we can also extract analogies and similarities that have a content of symbolic information useful for astrological interpretation; darkness, distance, and extreme density lead us to the idea of nuclear energy, lasers, television, microwaves, and microprocessors.

The fateful relationship of Pluto with death is only one side of the same coin. The other side relates it to the energy that activates life.

Pluto, like nuclear energy, is terrifyingly useful, especially to plutocrat countries, where the "much richer" rule. In this way, they keep the rest of the world terrified.

In its least fortunate aspect, Pluto is associated with terror, depravity, decay, perversion, vice, and hard lessons.

Pluto loves to stage its influence by terrorizing human beings. It is therefore associated with terrorism, whether from violent extremists, from ultra of any color, or the state. In politics, it has a direct relationship with populism, whether left or fascist.

Therefore, on a social level, it is related to all kinds of extremist or elitist groups, whose purpose is to achieve some kind of power, and to achieve their goals they use fear or terror, whether physical as in the case of ETA, IRA, Mafia, Al-Qaeda, Camorra, rulers of certain countries, or psychological as in the case of trade unionists, with their pickets, or the mass media.

From the small provincial newspaper to the major television networks, all those groups are capable of causing panic in our society. As happened in Rwanda in 1995, due to a radio station, where there was the most horrific massacre of the late 20th century.

Pluto is also associated with states of decomposition, fermentation, or extreme transformation.

In addition, due to its relationship with the underground world, it corresponds to volcanic eruptions and earthquakes, which also cause terror and panic.

Pluto is like a village at a dead end, where the comings and goings of its people allow them to find out what is happening in other villages, but the others do not know what is happening there. In such a way that the greed for information, knowledge, and power awakened by the astrological influence associated with Pluto, minimizes the curiosity of Mercury.

Pluto is the end, THE END, it's over, until here, this will be its behavior in astrological practice and when it arrives at a place we can say, it's over what was given.

Mythology and Symbolism of Pluto

Pluto was thought to be confined in the deepest and most remote part of the Earth's surface, from where he exerted his influence on crops and harvests. Both names, as well as their myths and symbolism, are useful to apply to this planet.

The original name of Pluto was Hades, meaning the idea of mystery and invisibility – very close to the reality of this planet –. The word Pluto comes from the root "wealth" and has a sense of hiding treasures under the ground. From the same root comes the word plutocracy, which means the government of the state in which power is in the hands of the rich and also refers to the richest class of a country that enjoys power or influence because of its wealth.

In Greek mythology, when the world was divided, he was assigned the kingdom of darkness, the underworld, the bosom of the earth that contains the dead or in transformation.

His most peculiar legend reveals the feminine aspect and precise information about its relationship with the signs of the zodiac. The myth tells that: in his kingdom of loneliness, Pluto felt the need to find a pleasant and beautiful companion (his moon, his feminine aspect). Eager to attract some lady, the king of the underworld put all his art into the development of his seduction techniques. But his passionate looks and his sweetened voice did nothing but provoke the laughter of the mocking goddesses.

–The desire to attract, passionate looks, and sweetened voice changes will be part of the archetypal baggage that will determine the behavioral patterns of people who are similar to this model–.

Tired and disillusioned with the Olympian goddesses, he hitched his carriage drawn by four black horses like ebony and headed for the fields of Sicily. Determined to find a companion, he traveled all over the island, until he reached a flowery field where the daughter of Demeter (the Mother Goddess, Nature) played with other nymphs, becoming the chosen one of his heart. The king of the underworld approached the young women timidly and at the feet of Persephone he declared his love.

At this point, the myth takes two paths: In some legends, it is narrated that Persephone went with him and ate a pomegranate seed in the kingdom of the depths, thus becoming linked to the underworld; while in others it is said that she said nothing in the face of Hades' demands, but transferred the decision to her mother, who denied this union for fear of losing her daughter forever. Faced with this attitude of her mother-in-law, Hades opted to kidnap Proserpina – the new name that Persephone takes when she joins Hades.

Demeter appealed to the justice of Zeus, her husband, and brother, to have her daughter returned to her. Hades also defended his rights before his brother Zeus. Demeter even threatened to say that as long as the separation from her daughter lasted, nature would cease to live on the surface of the earth and all the leaves of the trees would fall to the ground.

In the face of these pressures, Zeus decided that the fairest thing was for Persephone to live with her husband for one-third of the year, and the remaining two-thirds with her mother. Even so, Demeter maintained her position of not allowing any life outside during the annual separation period.

This part of the myth is related to the natural world's lifecycle and has several meanings. On the one hand, it represents the nine-month gestation period. -In the Homeric account, it is said that Demeter wandered the inhabited world for nine days, carrying flaming torches- This symbolizes the months of gestation again.

In a second interpretation, it tells the story of the natural world's lifecycle in our hemisphere. In a third interpretation, it provides information about astrological characteristics.

When the Sun leaves the sign of Scorpio, the leaves begin to fall. The life of nature is swallowed up into the earth. From this time on, the sowing of cereals and tubers begins −whose stems and leaves die in autumn but maintain their life underground−.

All agricultural or harvesting activities are related to what is found beneath the surface or linked to the collection of mushrooms. This passage from external life to inner life is linked to the mythical abduction of Persephone; in that period, in the sign of Pluto's domain, the abduction takes place, clearly showing the dominant sign of Pluto, its sign of active regency.

Four months later, that is, one−third of a year later, as the myth tells, the Sun enters the zodiac sign of Aries, Pluto's passive domicile. Here he is forced to give up his wife, he has to return his wife to the domains of his mother nature.

The entry of the Sun into Aries determines the beginning of spring; when the latent life below the surface bursts into the earth's crust to return

Persephone to the light. In Aries, Pluto has its second domicile, forming with Scorpio a circuit of life, death, and resurrection; what is absorbed by Scorpio is returned by Aries. Representing the cycle of perpetual rebirth.

The primordial model of Pluto in Aries is distinct from Pluto in Scorpio, where he appears absorbent, captivating, possessive, and conquering. The Scorpio model has a feminine behavior, like the sign; it takes from the outside and internalizes, where Pluto is the raptor, while in Aries a masculine model appears, which externalizes, takes from the inside out, experiences the sacrifice of the surrender of the loved one.

As in almost all myths, the first reading is referred to the cycles of nature. The four representations of the model represent the alternations of the seasons; three of them reside on the surface of the earth and one of them in the depths.

Core "the young", represents spring; Persephone, whose etymology is close to the idea of "radiance", is associated with summer; Proserpina, "the terrible", "the one who sacrifices the king", is related to autumn; and Hecate, goddess of the underworld, links to winter.

In another deeper, hidden reading, reserved for those who have already crossed the "clouds of the sanctuary" of the sphere of Daad; for those who have gone beyond the level of consciousness of Neptune; the myth reveals the secrets of immortality.

In the mythical account, Demeter begins the task of immortalizing Demophon by feeding him ambrosia and burying him among burning ashes at night.

The ambrosia, as Robert Graves develops, was composed of amanita muscaria, a mushroom that, according to Dioscorides, produces hallucinations, senseless frenzy, prophetic vision, erotic energy, and remarkable muscular strength.

In the plant world, the domain of Pluto encompasses all mushrooms, from the tasty mushroom to penicillin, passing through the deadly amanita muscaria, the Mexican "magic" or psycholybe mushrooms, etc.

Rober Graves continues by stating: *"The recipes cited by classical authors for nectar and cyceon, the mint-flavored drink that Demeter took in Eleusis, also formed the word 'mushroom'. I have eaten the hallucinogenic mushroom called psycholybe, a divine ambrosia used by the Mazatec Indians of the Oaxaca province in Mexico; I have heard the priestess invoke Tlaloc, the mushroom god, and I have seen transcendental visions."*

The burial among the burning ashes has a very special reading. For Chevalier, *"the ashes obtain their symbolism from the fact of being the residue of combustion, what remains after the extinction of the fire. For this reason, it means death and penance. The formula for Ash Wednesday is explicit: -You are dust, and to dust you shall return.*

By extension, it is therefore the consciousness of nothingness, of the nullity of the creature about the creator."

Another reading by the same author says: *"The ashes also indicate the return and internal combustion of seminal energy, which is one of the essential elements of tantric practices."*

The burning embers of this symbol are analogous to the annihilation of ecstasy, it is also the consciousness of nothingness concerning the Creator. But there is no ecstasy if there is no energy to provoke it.

Mushrooms, LSD, fasting techniques, staying in the dark, painful penances, and the most correct exercises are nothing more than the detonators of the internal combustion of seminal energy, associated with Pluto. The union of one of these detonators with seminal energy represents the completeness of the myth, and in all the mystical schools, forbidden to Puritans, they work beyond the sphere of Neptune.

Seminal energy, associated with Pluto, is the essential fuel without which, possibly St. Teresa would not have reached such a consciousness. In this symbolism, as in real life, experiences manifest themselves in all their aspects; the symbolism of ash contains death and penance, and both experiences are experienced when these states of consciousness are reached. Those who have experienced the experience of the "trip" know that they can find themselves with death and penance.

The archaic masculine representations of this model show us Pluto as the archetype of the severe human, with disheveled hair and a tense expression, wrapped in red robes. The classical model has a medium stature, and a robust build, with very delicate or fine skin and soft or thin hair.

As the only attribute, he wears the helmet of invisibility. The helmet is not only a symbol of invisibility, invulnerability, and power. The helmet covers Pluto's head, symbolizing the protection of thoughts, but it also hides them. It is therefore a symbol of invisibility that can become dissimulation. Perhaps because eroticism and sexual desire are things that must be hidden or disguised since Pluto is associated with the passion that awakens carnal love, exacerbated sexual love, and everything related to eroticism and sex.

The human model behaves with a passionate temperament, always with some resentment, generally self-destructive and solitary, with a perceptive penetrating mind that breaks the established schemes. He is tremendously susceptible, gets angry at anything, loves secrets, and is recognized by his eyes that come out of their sockets leaving a little white above and below.

In the human body, it is related to the skin, thyroid, pores, perianal area, anus, and buttocks.

Keywords of Pluto

Character-Destiny

Amoral-Disappearances of all kinds

Passionate-Hard and unsatisfactory events

Ultralogical-Ecologists and extremist groups

Self-sufficient-Deep transformations

Insatiable-Situations of limits, breaking of schemes

Enigmati-Obsessive experiences

Susceptible-Desires and ambitions for power

Melikerionic-Power and Plutocracy

Explanation

Pluto is the dwarf planet that rules the sign of Scorpio. It is associated with power, transformation, and death. The keywords listed above describe the qualities and experiences that are often associated with Pluto.

Amoral

Pluto is often seen as amoral, meaning that it does not follow traditional moral codes. This can be seen in the way that Pluto is associated with death, destruction, and violence. However, it can also be seen in the way that Pluto is associated with transformation and change. Pluto is not afraid to break down old structures to create new ones.

Passionate

Pluto is also associated with passion. This passion can be seen in the intensity of Pluto's emotions, as well as in the intensity of its desires. Pluto people are often driven by their passions, and they are not afraid to go after what they want.

Urological

Pluto is also associated with ultralogic, meaning that it thinks outside the box. Pluto people are often very creative and innovative, and they are not afraid to challenge the status quo.

Self-sufficient

Pluto is also associated with self-sufficiency. Pluto people are often very independent and self-reliant. They do not need others to validate them, and they are comfortable being on their own.

Insatiable

Pluto is also associated with insatiable desires. Pluto people are often very ambitious, and they are always looking for new challenges. They are never satisfied with the status quo, and they are always striving for something more.

Enigmatic

Pluto is also associated with being enigmatic. Pluto people are often very mysterious and secretive. They can be difficult to understand, and they often keep their true feelings hidden.

Susceptible

Pluto is also associated with being susceptible to power. Pluto people are often drawn to power, and they can be easily corrupted by it. They need to be careful not to let their ambitions get the best of them.

Melikerionic

The word "melikerionic" is a Greek word that means "loving power." It is a term that is often used to describe Pluto people. Pluto people are often very passionate about power, and they can be very effective leaders. However, they need to be careful not to abuse their power.

Objects and Places

Television

Toilets, WC, Loo

Lavatory, Latrine

Trash can

Basements and cellars

Places born from nothing

Isolated places

Islands and volcanoes

Cemeteries

Symbolism of Lilith

Lilith is one of the most enigmatic and misunderstood astrological archetypes of all celestial models, especially misunderstood by many people who are in the process of integrating the model.

– Let's analyze the origin, meaning, and content of this archetype to better understand it and help with its integration into the personality:

– The name Lilith comes from Hebrew tradition, Lil, which means night, darkness, twilight, and also a disastrous time and calamity. On the other hand, Lilith means owl, the bird with which Palas Athena is represented in Greek culture, as in a certain way she competes with her in seeing in the dark.

However, Athena uses technology, while Lilith employs more subtle methods.

The first known image of Lilith appears as a beautiful, winged, and naked woman, with bird feet, standing on top of two lions and flanked by a pair of owls. Her name also means Queen of the she-demons, and in the same way, Lilah refers to the color lilac, a color often used by women possessed by this archetype during times of empowerment.

People who are "attacked" by this model always wear some purple or lilac garment. Many women even wear this color on the color of their lips.

In Hebrew mythology, it is said that she was the first woman, created at the same time as Adam, but not from one of his ribs, as is related in Genesis 2/22, but at the same time as Adam, directly from the earth, as it says in Genesis 1/27.

"And God created man in his image, in the image of God created he him; male and female created he them," I repeat, male and female, as it is written in

the original Hebrew. In Hebrew mythology, Lilith is known as the first woman, anterior to Eve.

For the Hebrews, Lilith is the rebellious model of a woman who refuses to submit to her husband, she is the enemy of Eve and represents the instigator of illegitimate loves, the perturbator of the marital bed.

Lilith refused to submit to her husband and left him, she says to Adam: "We are equal, since we come from the earth!" When she says this, disagreements and disagreements arise, but in reality the dispute is about who should have greater authority.

In the Jewish Encyclopedia, it is said that *"Lilith considered the reclining position that he required offensive. Why should I lie under you? I was also made of dust, and therefore I am your equal."*

It is said that the couple never found peace, mainly because Lilith, not wanting to renounce her equality, argued with her partner about the way and the form of carrying out their carnal union.

The Sumerians and Babylonians considered her as a being that inhabits the unconscious world of dreams. For them she was a succubus who visited men in their dreams, from this relationship faceless monsters were born; she also had many servants who similarly tried to seduce men in their dreams.

She was therefore the princess of the succubi, a seducer and devourer of men.

While the Greeks knew this same archetype as Pandora, the first woman created by Zeus who ordered Hephaestus to wet earth and water to create mud, and form a beautiful virgin's body, thus creating the first woman; he also requested the collaboration of Athena – the Wisdom – who lent her garments and girdled her with her belt; Hermes transferred his qualities to her and Aphrodite anointed her forehead with grace and persuasion.

It is worth remembering that in Greek mythology, Pandora was created as punishment for men.

This feminine archetype is not exclusive to women. Jung says that in men, the feminine aspect is personified in the unconscious by the anima, and women also have an animus. He argues that there is a biological basis for these sexual opposites. In every man, there is a majority of male genes and a minority of female genes. The anima corresponds to the minority of women in men, and vice versa.

Only the integration of the personality can be achieved through the anima for men and the animus in women, as these figures constitute the autonomous personification of the unconscious for both sexes.

Jung's concept of the anima and animus is based on his theory of the collective unconscious. The collective unconscious is a reservoir of inherited memories and archetypes that are shared by all humans. The anima is the feminine archetype in men, and the animus is the masculine archetype in women.

According to Jung, the anima and animus are important for the development of the personality. They represent the unconscious aspects of the personality, and they can be a source of creativity, inspiration, and insight.

In the case of men, the anima can represent the feminine side of their personality. It can include qualities such as intuition, creativity, and emotionality. When a man integrates his anima, he becomes more whole and balanced.

In the case of women, the animus can represent the masculine side of their personality. It can include qualities such as strength, logic, and ambition. When a woman integrates her animus, she becomes more self-reliant and assertive.

The integration of the anima and animus is a lifelong process. It can be achieved through psychotherapy, dreams, and other forms of self-exploration.

The influence of this archetype in men, when it is poorly integrated or in the integration phase, can be perceived as a certain degree of "effeminacy" that stands out with greater or lesser intensity according to the evolution of each person, while in women a degree of "masculinity" can be appreciated and a greater capacity for decision and independence.

In addition to the complexes that come from repressed sexuality, some complexes come directly from the unconscious. The greater the repressed energy, the stronger will be the power of attraction of this archetype, which can be a source of strength, the "genius" of an individual, and also the "demon" that possesses it. The reason for the power of this demon lies in the fact that the autonomous complex emerges from the unconscious and identifies itself with the Ego, without the person attacked being able to distinguish it from his conscious attitude.

The archetype of Lilith can be recognized as the shadow that is difficult to integrate, a model that contains the unacceptable, the repressed, or the difficult to assume.

Lilith, as Chevalier says, cannot be integrated into the frameworks of human existence, of interpersonal and community relationships, she is rejected to the abyss of the unconscious, from where she does not cease to induce desire that moves away from social and family norms. For this same author, Lilith's home is fixed in the depths of the sea, from where monsters arise; a symbol of the subconscious, where the censorship of consciousness seeks to prevent it from coming out so that it does not come to disturb the lives of men and women of the earth.

Pandora of the Greeks is the Lilith that symbolizes the origin of the evils of humanity, it is the box of repressions and the symbol of what should not be opened. But in its positive aspect, it is also the vase of hope that hides in that deep unconscious, where all possibilities, all riches, and all desires are latent.

This astrological model is a gravitational force, absent of consciousness that is disguised as wisdom but that contains the desire to have greater authority and to establish itself as a dominant figure, this archetype survives in the world of dreams, especially in those dreams that have an impudent content.

Lilith is an archetype that cannot be integrated into the framework of ordinary life, as it engenders ghostly creatures and incites curiosity. However, its integration into the personality as a whole facilitates victory, increases prosperity, and improves eloquence.

When the archetype of Lilith takes over the consciousness of a woman or a man, after having been long repressed, one enters fully into what is known as the "paranoid" world.

This dark aspect of consciousness, almost always unacceptable or unacceptable is what is projected without prior notice, breaking into certain personal experiences, in the form of moods or impulses that lead to actions that later cannot be explained or excused.

The irruption of Lilith into consciousness or life is perceived as if another individual appropriated the personality to do, say, or think a series of things as opposed to the will of the conscious ego. Jung describes the projection of the shadow onto others, as the weaknesses and defects that are not accepted, all the bad and inferior qualities that are not recognized, are projected into the shadow of others.

Another aspect of personality attributable to poorly integrated Lilith is suspicion and sidelong glances. She is the woman who acts as if she wants to detect some conspiracy, she shows herself with a suspicious thought, rigidity, attention constantly directed towards investigative activities, hypersensitivity to criticism, and behavioral patterns such as suspicion, hostility, or arrogance.

Poorly integrated Lilith, that is, repressed for years, usually causes a transformation of loving feelings into experiences of hatred and persecution. When it increases in pressure due to its repression, an insidious development of a persistent and unshakable delusional system ends up occurring, while at the same time the clarity and order of thought, will, and action are preserved.

The woman (or man) trapped by Lilith is a hypervigilant observer who does not make extravagant conjectures; she investigates and carefully examines what is around her, lacks humor that she may feel is humiliating, does not entertain her, and also interprets it as something ridiculous. On the other hand, a strong fascination appears for hidden meanings and any event that goes beyond the ordinary suggests an extraordinary explanation to her.

The poorly integrated Lilith woman presents a characteristic trait an inability to forget and forgive, and she is usually vengeful. Her ability to find defects is highly developed, as she becomes more personally committed, she feels more threatened.

In outbreaks of uncontrolled behavior, she is confused and often describes the feeling that "something strange is happening" and experiences feelings of depersonalization and becomes distrustful, argumentative, and hypersensitive in her interpersonal relationships.

She maintains a defensive attitude whose two main weapons are mistrust and excessive aggressiveness. Her intellectual performance is often above average since she dedicates all her effort to keeping her faculties under control, she usually has hypermnesia, although it is an increase in memory influenced by her motivations. Lilith, being a feminine model, is more active in a certain type of women who have the feeling of being the center of interest of others, they are women who easily take offense or feel underestimated, they possess, in most cases, an unjustified pride or an aspect of self-sufficiency.

The Lilith woman is cautious, cares about hidden motivations and meanings, and exaggerates her autonomy. She has the feeling of being different and usually gets involved in some "crusade" against social injustice.

-Lilith is poorly integrated makes you feel uncomfortable working "under" others, has a conflict with the authority figure and a hyper-acuteness to sensations – often pleasant – and always has auditory illusions, hears internal voices that she does not associate with consciousness, and prefers to maintain an argumentative and provocative attitude, they choose to argue, rather than yield. Just like the original archetype.

In another sense, Lilith is the mistress of witchcraft, the witch that we all carry within us – women and men – or the shadow of the anima or animus, if we want to use psychological language. It is the archetype that tries to establish itself as the dominant one; it is the vindicatory model, the one that rebels against all kinds of inequalities, so it is not the dominant archetype, it is the competitor of the conscious ego, which is projected into social attitudes. However, it is Lilith who has a deep knowledge of the energies that govern the body.

When Lilith is well integrated, it brings grace and persuasion to the personality, and adds the power of decision and responsibility; but when it is completely repressed, it is the provoker of paranoid syndromes and full of projections such as impudence, falsehood, or perfidy and develops a punishing, enveloping and dominant personality.

The influence of poorly integrated Lilith generates a tendency to polemicize, and forces others to clarify their positions both in terms of various topics and relation to her; she has to decide to take sides. She feels more comfortable in front of a well-identified enemy than in front of a person whose position is not clearly defined. She seems anxious to discover a social injustice and then channel her anger to rectify it. She is eager to "teach people a lesson." Her strength lies in her repression.

When this model is assumed or well-integrated, a splendid prototype of a woman appears, as described by Manuela Dum in her book of the Goddesses.

"The woman Circe has dared to look within and illuminate a wild force that, in reality, all women share... Her magic consists of the ability to establish herself as the dominant one... The woman Circe lives in her magical world and invites others to participate in her witchcraft. She is the kind of woman who welcomes others warmly, inspiring a sense of warmth that makes them open their hearts and reveal their secrets to her courteous ear. Her presence and manners can cause an alchemical transformation in other people."

For example, she can make others feel comfortable and in touch with their own instincts. The woman Circe usually possesses a deep knowledge of the energies that govern the body; she could be a doctor, acupuncturist, or physiotherapist."

To integrate the Lilith model is equivalent to assuming nakedness and accepting those primitive impulses as a part, although it is the dark part, the furthest from consciousness, but a part of our personality. It is the work of the astrologer and the psychologist to illuminate this aspect of consciousness, to clarify and facilitate the individual's knowledge of this dark archetype through which one must pass to achieve the integration of the personality.

"The best therapy is a week at the Vera Natura Hotel in Almeria or any other similar place."

A Female Model for Aries

Like any zodiac sign, Aries, in addition to containing an archetype related to the planet Mars, which is markedly masculine, must contain a pattern of female behavior, not in vain Pluto has a female or internal regency in this sign.

Mars is born from the union between Deus piter and Deus meter, that is, between God the Father and Goddess the Mother, Jupiter and Demeter. From the same union, that is, from the same parents, Kore the young woman is born, who will later be the wife of Pluto.

Perhaps for many this name does not mean anything, but Kore the young woman, who is the personification of spring, will change her name when Hades kidnaps her. Then she will be called Persephone and later Proserpina, perhaps she is better known by these names.

Let's review a little of the first part, the part of Aries, of the most famous myth. Kore with her nymphs did not think about men or glory, they dedicated themselves to frolicking among themselves, to having fun dancing and they were always smiling.

They were very vital beings who adored life, especially spring.

They could be seen playing like crazy, they made crowns and belts of flowers for which they felt a childish passion, they were charming and funny beings.

They adorned their dresses with saffron, iris, and hyacinth flowers.

These ornaments allow us to deduce that they were very active at the beginning of spring.

Kore gathered her nymphs and they would launch themselves in groups, holding hands, running wildly, and then they would lie down on the fragrant grass and fill their baskets with roses and violets.

It was precisely the contemplation of this ingenuous and delicious spectacle that attracted Hades. Legend has it that one day Kore was with several nymphs of her entourage taking a bath and frolicking on the shore of a small lake in the center of Sicily and when he saw them Hades felt tremendously passionate and threw himself on the group of nymphs.

All the nymphs ran to seek refuge in the nearby forests, mad with fear and horrified by the presence of the god, all fled in terror, all sought refuge except Kore, who did not move a single eyelash because she was focused on her own thing, very entertained looking and absorbing the aroma of a beautiful narcissus flower.

The distracted Kore was about to cut the flower when she felt someone take her in their arms and take her away. To defend herself, the poor woman had no other weapons than her cries and tears. How many tears did she shed and what cries of despair came from her heart? But her laments and cries instead of softening the heart of her kidnapper, excited him more and increased his desire for the goddess.

At the end of this chapter, Kore, exhausted by the pain and fear, faded away in the arms of Hades. When she wakes up she is no longer Kore, from that moment on she will be called Persephone.

After the kidnapping, Persephone had to change her environment for a time, and she found herself surrounded by Hades' court, which was composed of a small group of infernal divinities.

So she was a companion of the three Fates, one of them called Clotho, the one with a spinning wheel with wool, silk, and gold to spin the days of man's life, the other two help her in the task by turning the use to extract the thread and another cut it with scissors; indicating in this way the birth, duration, and end of man's life.

They are known as the Fates because they are granting an instant of life more than decreed.

She was also in the company of Fury, who had a bloody head, and a disfigured face, surrounded by weapons and tearing apart chains.

She was also accompanied by Hatred, biting her lips with a perfidious smile, but simulated.

She was hypocritical, covering her evil and ugly face with a mask of benign appearance.

Betrayal, smiling, presenting a sprig of olive with her right hand and hiding a dagger with her left.

Revenge, hiding among roses a smoking torch and some intertwined snakes.

Among the entire court of her abductor, Death was also present, Hades' favorite until then, dressed in a black crepe cloak spangled with stars and holding a scythe in her right hand.

From this review of her mythology, we can extract a model that must have some natural patterns of behavior and others that may have become attached due to its contact with other models or at least has known and therefore awareness of what these issues are.

The crazy races holding hands with a group of nymphs, from the myth of Kore, suggests a very spontaneous, fresh optimistic, active, and fun behavior model.

"Kore with her nymphs did not think about men or glory." – This female model in its first part of life, adopts a behavior model that has little inclination towards affairs with men, in her youth she is oblivious to ambitions of glory and romantic conquest, this archetype inclines her to run around with her group, to play and have fun without caring too much about other topics.

"They lay on the fragrant grass and filled their baskets with roses and violets."

From this paragraph, it can be deduced that the female Korean model seeks solace, peace, and tranquility outside of cities, that she likes nature, and that she loves flowers, colors, and the aromas they give off. Perhaps that is why they have a very sensitive sense of smell. –The sense of smell is the first sense, the deepest of the senses, the fifth sense, the closest to the sixth sense, which is intuition. Perhaps this archetype, because it has a lot of smell, has a good chance of awakening that sixth sense.

"All the nymphs ran to seek refuge in the nearby forests, mad with fear and horrified by the presence of the god, all fled in terror, all sought refuge except Kore, who did not move even an eyelash because she was in her own thing, very entertained looking and absorbing the aroma of a beautiful narcissus flower."

Everyone runs away but the female Aries model does not. It does not even occur to her to think that she has or must flee from anything, she is in her own thing, smelling the scent of the narcissus.

The narcissus is a symbol associated with this model, which means that possibly in the Aries woman there is a hint of what the narcissus means.

In case anyone has forgotten, I will tell you the myth of Narcissus:

Narcissus was a handsome young man, the son of the river Cephisus and the nymph Liriope. They say that this young man was indifferent to the feelings of love that he awakened in the nymphs. Apparently, Cupid had accumulated many failures with the young man, and, desperate after so many setbacks, he devised a very special punishment. One day when Narcissus was sleeping under a tree on the shore of a pond, Cupid shot him with a golden arrow and pierced his heart.

—I assume you know that Cupid has two types of arrows, one gold and one lead. Whoever is shot with a golden arrow falls madly in love with the first person they see, and whoever is shot with a lead arrow feels the opposite and feels a deep contempt for the first person they meet.

Well, he shot Narcissus with a golden arrow and when he woke up, he went to wash his face with the water from the pond and saw his reflection on the crystal-clear water. When he saw himself, he fell madly in love with himself. In the end, the gods took pity on him and transformed him into the flower called Narcissus.

Perhaps the Aries model, whether female or male, contains a certain degree of narcissism, but at the same time, it is a model that adores life. They are charming and funny beings who do not flee out of distraction and who at the same time end up hearing their cries of despair or their laments and groans.

This pure pattern, which cannot be fully given in any person, I think would also be noticeable in women who have Pluto in the angles, next to the Sun, or receiving a closed aspect from this planet. If the aspect is soft, this pattern will integrate easily, but if the Pluto aspect is tense, they may claim me for my audacity.

A Female Model for Capricorn

In this zodiac sign, the pattern of behavior associated with Saturn is known and accepted by all, but Santa Claus is a masculine pattern of behavior, and although women also resonate with that model, it is not possible that the ancients had forgotten the female model of Saturn.

In mythology, or in what we could call "theology of the ancient gods," something similar happens to what happens in theology, especially when we talk about God and His Son, where it is said that they are the same person. In mythological theology, the same thing also happens with certain divinities such as Demeter and her daughter Persephone, or with

Saturn and his daughter Hestia, who later became Vesta.

This goddess, the model of behavior or female archetype, was already known since antiquity and was applied as regent in the sign of Capricorn, or at least this is what can be thought when reading Manilius in his Astronomicón, who assigns Vesta as regent of Capricorn.

Vesta of the Romans is the Hestia of the Greeks. Let's review a bit of her mythology and thus we can compare it with the patterns of female behavior applicable to Capricorn or to certain types of Saturnine women with whom this pattern of behavior resonates.

According to Hesiod, Hestia was the first daughter of Saturn, the firstborn among the seven children of Saturn, sister of Demeter, Hades, Zeus, and Poseidon.

In this first encounter with the model, we find ourselves before an older sister who must exercise the function of "the most responsible" and has to take care of household tasks to replace or help in the work of the mother or organizer of the home and also has to keep the central fire of the house. Perhaps that is why she was considered the goddess of the hearth.

She received worship in the Prytaneion, which was the common home of Athens where the sacred fire of the hearth was kept. Think about a time when there was no butane gas, no electric stoves, no bic lighters, no matches, no tobacconists where you could buy them, and even less so, gentlemen who pass by on the street and you ask them for fire. Keeping the fire was an extremely important task that also forced you to be centered in the home.

For this reason, Vesta represents the inner and central fire that distills the Capricornian pattern of behavior. Where else does that fiery personality of Capricornian women come from? Yes, it is true, this sign also has the exaltation of Mars, but one thing does not cancel out the other, but rather complements it.

Several representations of the model are known, in which sometimes she is seated and sometimes standing, but always in complete immobility, just as she was conceived because she was located in the immobile center of the world.

From this we can extract another pattern of behavior; immobility and centralism. If we stretch these concepts a little, we can conclude that within this model of behaviors, there is a tendency to position oneself in the center and stay there.

In the palace of Justiniano in Rome, there is an image that represents her standing, dressed simply in a tunic that falls to her feet. She has her head, chest, and back covered by a veil similar to that of Isis −in the end, they are sisters− The right arm down and back, as if pointing to the earth, and the left at the height of the head, pointing to the sky. It is an image of a serene, calm, serious, and dignified religious appearance.

The Romans, just as they do with Zeus, Jupiter, or Cronos−Saturn, changed the name of Hestia to

Vesta. Vesta retains the same attributes as the goddess of the sacred fire and the home. In Rome, she had the same hierarchy of homes as Hestia in Greece. Cato recommended keeping the domestic home clean, taking a walk around it every night before going to bed, and bringing Vesta a wreath of flowers three times a month.

From this, we can extract another pattern of behavior that is recognized in the role of keeping the house clean and taking a little walk around the home before going to bed, when everyone has already gone to sleep. Do Capricornian women do this?

This goddess had at her disposal an entire caste of women who served her as her priestesses, known as the Vestals. They had to be girls between six and ten years old and belong to a noble or free social class, never of slave origin. They also could not have any physical defects. This same caste and cult survives in a place that is par excellence Capricornian, one of the most mountainous places in the world where those same goddess-girls and that same cult still exist. Here we once again observe how these old gods and goddesses receive worship today.

The Vestals took care of the sacred fire, which must never be extinguished because this fire represented the course of the empire. If the fire ever went out, the Vestals would receive severe beatings.

From these paragraphs, we can also extract patterns of behavior that are hinted at in Capricornian women. How many Capricornian women have been physically or psychologically punished for letting their inner fire go out and denying their sexuality to their partner?

The Vestals had to remain completely celibate, and both adulteresses and men who abused them were sentenced to death. But the death sentence reserved for the Vestals had a horrible peculiarity, as they were forced to descend into their tomb, and were locked up with an oil lamp, some water, bread, and milk so that they died of starvation.

Here we see a dark pattern of behavior that threatens the behavior of those who are subject to this model. But it also has the counterpart that the Vestals who fulfilled their duty to maintain the fire received multiple honors. All the magistrates and of course the rest of the people, gave way to them. Their word was worthy of credit in the trials. All state secrets were entrusted to them and they were also reserved the best seat in the circuses. In addition, their expenses were the responsibility of the State for life.

Manuela Dunn, in her book of the Goddesses – a beautiful book published in Spanish by Robonbook/Círculo de lectores – describes female models most exquisitely, among those models she also exposes that Vesta, from which I am going to extract some paragraphs that I find extraordinary.

"The archetype of Vesta represents the inner wisdom of a woman. Like a priestess, the Vesta woman understands every event in her life, every circumstance, as a spiritual lesson through which she learns to transcend the world.

Her ego has not dissolved as others would like to believe, but exists coldly in the denial of the self. She would be the kind of woman who congratulates herself for not reacting to something that hurts her or makes her happy because that shows that she is beyond human imperfection and that nothing moves her because she is focused on her path.

Her cordiality with men is on the verge of the impersonal, which can give them the impression that she is a free woman. She leaves a wide margin in the relationship to allow them to do what they want. She may appear to not care that her man goes with another woman because she believes that there is always another lesson to learn about detachment, even though her heart breaks inside her.

This kind of thing is what irritates other women, who may believe that she denies her true feelings and is not sincere with her loved one by giving him a false impression. In addition, other women can detect the loneliness and sadness that this role produces in them.

One of the main themes of the Vesta woman is her solitude, which she values highly. When the Vesta woman recognizes her humanity and finds the courage to be completely honest about her feelings, sharing her solitude, sadness, happiness, and even bad mood with others, the true wisdom of the archetype is revealed.

She is an imaginative and tender lover, as well as a good friend and counselor and the best companion for a man.

The Vesta archetype can be activated by doing domestic work calmly and without haste. Even the most extroverted woman discovers that there are times when cleaning, placing flowers in a vase, ironing, putting clothes away in lavender-scented drawers, and embroidering a pillowcase are sources of relaxation and excellent activities for finding oneself. Caring for the house as if performing a Vesta honor ritual can invest us with serenity and gratitude, as if we were cleansing our spirit of outside influences, focusing on ourselves and peace of mind."

I understand that after reading the Vesta model by the pen of Manuela Dunn, I have almost nothing left to say about the Capricorn woman model.

A Female Model for Aquarius

I am not the first, nor the discoverer of a new feminine model for Aquarius. Other astrologers have already introduced a feminine model for this zodiac sign, such as Lilly Süllos. For this author, the sign of Aquarius is the unmistakable abode of the goddess Pallas Athena. I agree with her and I think it is appropriate to offer my opinion on this feminine model of Aquarius. Other astrologers give Pallas the regency in Aries, especially Manilius, who advocates for the regency of Juno.

The regency of the planet Uranus in the sign of Aquarius is accepted by the vast majority of astrologers, without eliminating its classical regency of Saturn. With Saturn, it is easy to develop a masculine model using traditional mythology, but with Uranus, it is fruitless to use the same classical mythology since this name was imposed outside the cultural context and at a much later time. The name Uranus was given to it by the astronomer Johan Bode, its theoretical discoverer along with Daniel Titus, who proposed the law now known as Titus-Bode's law or Bode's law. These laws allow us to predict the existence of a new planet in the place where Herschel observed what he believed to be a comet.

Some astrologers maintain that Uranus is like the eighth superior of Mercury, while others speak of Uranus in terms of electricity and violence. If we make a show of syncretism, it could be said that the most similar typical model would be represented by an intermediate archetype between Mars and Mercury.

Due to the lack of luminosity of the planet, it would be necessary to add dark traits, that is, symbolically feminine. In this way, the model of

Pallas Athena fits perfectly. Many astrologers have perfectly integrated this archetype.

But let's get to know a little about this surprising feminine model. Pallas Athena has several legends about her birth. The last known one tells that her father was the giant Pallas (son of the Earth) who tried to rape her, because of it, the goddess killed him, skinned him, and with his skin made the aegis (breastplate of virginity). To seal her victory, she assumed the warrior name of Pallas Athena.

In another legend, she is associated with Poseidon (Neptune), perhaps because of her zodiac sign neighborhood; Uranus or Pallas rules the sign of Aquarius and Neptune the neighboring sign of Pisces. On the other hand, Neptune is the divinity that dominates the liquid element of the seas, while Pallas, born on the shores of a lake, symbolizes the lightning that precedes the rains; Aquarius precedes Pisces.

But the most well-known legend considers her the daughter of Zeus and Metis (wisdom). It is said that Metis was Zeus's first lover. Metis being pregnant, Gea and Uranus told Zeus that after giving him a daughter, Metis would give him a son who would dethrone him, as he had dethroned Cronus. Then Zeus swallowed Metis, who was carrying Athena in her womb. Shortly after, Zeus felt severe headaches, so severe that they became so unbearable that he begged Hephaestus to relieve them in any way. Hephaestus according to some or Prometheus according to others, opened his skull with his bronze sword. Through the open wound and giving a prolonged cry of victory, Athena emerged; clad in shining armor and brandishing a steel javelin. Seeing her, a feeling of respect and awe-filled all the immortals. The vast Olympus was shaken by the impetuous emergence of the goddess with the shining eyes. -Those big and shining eyes that we will always see in the women who represent the model-. She was called "the goddess with the glaucus eyes."

Athena is a chaste divinity, she never lets herself be carried away by her love impulse, which contrasts curiously with the rest of the inhabitants of Olympus. Despite the slanderous insinuations about her supposed relationships with Helios, Hercules, and Hephaestus, of whom it is said that he tried to rape her.

This divinity has a belligerent and warlike character, she surpasses even the god of war. Although she only used it to help the heroes worthy of her compassion.

The fact of being born out of the head of Zeus places her as the goddess of intelligence, but she was also a war goddess and, as Juan B. Bergua recounts, a Hippia, that is, a horse tamer. In reality, Athena teaches men to domesticate nature using ingenuity and shows them how to use the horse bridle, although her favorite animal is the owl.

She was the protective divinity of the Acropolis and the guardian of the cities. She lived in the heights that had strategic importance. Athena presided over all the arts and works of peace. She was also known by the epithet of Ergane "the industrious worker". There was a proverb in the weaving workshops of Athens that said "Moving the fingers with the help of Athena" In this way, it indicated her mastery in all works.

She was also the patroness of potters, for she, along with Hephaestus, was the one who modeled Pandora, the first figure of a woman, to whom she left with the resources necessary to seduce men. But she was above all the goddess of reason and wisdom, for this reason, she personifies reflective thought.

The most famous representation is the Athena of the Parthenon, a work by Phidias. She is covered in a long tunic, and wears a helmet on her head, and her chest the aegis; her right arm rests on the javelin or lance, and her right hand holds a winged victory.

From this way of dressing and these attributes, we can extract some behavioral patterns that define the model:

The tunic that covers her body marks a notable difference from the other divinities that generally go uncovered, this concealment of the body possibly symbolizes the impossibility of viewing the planet with which it is associated, and also represents a model of chaste or not voluptuous woman, or who prefers not to be provocative for fear of being sexually assaulted, as happens to Athena.

The spear is a masculine symbol and indicates strength and authority. In legal activities, it represented the protection of contracts, processes, and debates. In this model, it also means strength and authority in its environment, in its environment, with its family and friends.

The aegis, at first symbolized the storm that generates terror and panic, but contrary to the lightning bolt, it is not a weapon designed to strike, but rather a psychological weapon that intends to inspire fear and incite mortals not to put their trust in anyone but those who deserve it, as Chevalier recounts. The woman Athena enjoys scaring, alarming, and surprising others.

The helmet is a symbol of invisibility, invulnerability, and power. The helmet of Athena, like that of Pluto, made whoever wore it invisible. The helmet protects by making it invisible. When Athena came to the aid of Diomedes to fight Ares, she wore the helmet that characterized her. The woman Athena acts invisibly, she protects herself by pretending to be "Swedish", distracted, as if she had never broken a plate in her life.

From this symbolic baggage, a pure model of a woman can be formed, but this pure model can hardly be found in a person, as is the case with any of the other models.

Certainly, Athena is a very enigmatic model, a model of a chaste or less voluptuous woman who never lets herself be swayed by her amorous impulse or sees male sexuality as aggression. This anomaly must have its explanation because, in her myths, there are several situations where someone tries to violate her. This could be associated with a model of a woman who has suffered an attempted rape or sexual assault and has developed a protective armor to defend herself against such eventualities.

In the myth, it is narrated that the other gods were overwhelmed, as they say, that seeing her filled all immortals with a feeling of respect and astonishment. Therefore, the woman Athena must have characteristics that inspire respect and surprise. Generally, her large eyes are highlighted, which resemble the image of the goddess with shining eyes. The woman Athena stands out because of her eyes, her penetrating gaze that seems to see everything, and her large and open way of looking that makes us feel that she discovers everything we carry inside.

The woman Athena confronts life with a psychological weapon that aims to inspire respect and surprise, qualities that allow her to incite others. Athena is decidedly inciting and strategic, she usually does not act, or if she does, she does it by deploying her strategy, like generals, from a high or invisible place. Athena moves or stimulates others to do things, but she stays on the sidelines, playing innocently.

The personality of Athena has traits of a combatant, she doesn't shy away from contradicting and confronting those who disagree with her. She can even take delight in her defensive actions, which denotes a degree of cruelty, as in the archetype. They are always women who display an authoritarian disposition and a strong character, enough to compete with or challenge men for any social or professional position. Their weapons are strategy, wit, and their secret resources to seduce others.

Manuela Dunn, in her book "The Goddesses", presents a model of Athena that is worth knowing:

"Women who are aligned with the archetype of Athena may be, for example, successful investors who can instinctively detect market movements and act accordingly, planning the timing and strategy. They may also be brilliant professionals, able to unravel the intricacies of corporate politics and internal competition. The Athena woman possesses the gift of logical thinking, which is intuitive. She can keep her mind clear amid powerful emotions and provide practical solutions to complex problems. The Athena woman is an impartial judge, as the myth says; she can be an excellent professional counselor or business advisor, providing companies with carefully crafted management programs.

Always flanked by powerful heroes and gods, Athena can seem "masculine" and also very mature. She undoubtedly possesses a moral and psychological integrity that is very different from that of any other goddess. Her wisdom is practical, her tactics are cold and resolute, and her gift for *strategy implies that she is aware of ethics and diplomacy; so she knows power and respects it. As a result, an Athena woman may be misunderstood by other women, as she is not considered to be "feminine" enough.*

Powerful men often trust women with the qualities of Athena and seek their advice. In her later years, the Athena woman may well be almost a magician, a strategist of destiny who advises others how to advance in their own projects towards the achievement of a fulfilling life."

What Manuela Dunn does not tell us is what Athena does with her feelings, where are her emotions, how she expresses her affections, and where has her sensuality gone. And that is a mystery that only Athenas can reveal to us...

A Female Model for Virgo. Isis-Demeter

We have assumed that each stretch of sky is divided into sectors and each sector has a different and particular symbolic content. In the sign of Cancer, the symbolism and archetypes associated with the Moon were very relevant, in Leo the solar archetype manifests itself more clearly, and in Virgo —here there may be discrepancies— the earthly model is expressed.

The Earth is the mother planet that shelters us. From a general point of view, it is distinguished from the other celestial bodies in our system, because the phenomenon of organic and intelligent life appears on its crust.

From the symbolic point of view, it can be associated with the symbolism and the archetype of Isis – the mother of nature in Egyptian culture – then we will link this model with the Demeter of the Greeks and Ceres of the Romans until we associate it with the black virgins of Christian mythology.

For the ancients, Isis was a representation of the fertile and cultivated land, she was the model of love for life, the virgin mother who gives life and health to humans. Her myth tells that she helped men in their work of civilization by teaching women to grind grain, spin flax, and weave fabrics; she taught how to cure diseases and accustomed them to live in families, instituting marriage for this purpose.

With the expression that "Every living being has a drop of blood of Isis", one wants to remember the materiality of nature in all living beings on the planet, including humans. Plutarch writes that her older brother, Osiris, chose her as his wife; since then she sat beside him on the throne of the living. During the absence of her husband, who had peacefully gone to conquer the world, Isis ruled with prudence as regent.

Isis-Demeter is a powerful archetype that can be a source of inspiration for women of all ages. She represents the power of nature, the love of life, and the wisdom of the ages. Women who identify with this archetype are often nurturing, compassionate, and wise. They are also often drawn to careers in healing, teaching, or social work.

Here are Some of the Key Qualities of the Isis-Demeter Archetype:

Nurturing: Isis Demeter is the mother of nature, and she is deeply connected to the cycle of life and death. She is a symbol of unconditional love and support.

Compassionate: Isis-Demeter is a wise and compassionate goddess. She is always willing to help those in need.

Wise: Isis-Demeter is a symbol of wisdom and knowledge. She is a teacher and a guide.

Osiris was killed and dismembered by his brother Set, – the genius of evil – who fragmented his body into numerous pieces (reminding us of the explosion and subsequent fragmentation of the planet Phaethon, now the asteroid belt), and dispersed them in the most remote corners of the world.

Isis searched until she found the precious remains, which she patiently reunited and, with her magical practices, managed to revive him enough to conceive a child with him. This is why she is also depicted with a child in her arms, later associated with pre-Christian black virgins. These virgins, like the ancient Isis, were worshipped in the deepest and most feminine aspects of the earth, such as the Black Virgin of Monserrat, worshipped inside a cave. Or as is the case with Notre Dame de Meymac.

The archetype of Isis is none other than what the Roman Church transmitted to us with the name of the Virgin Mary, the Virgin Mother, associated with her domicile in the zodiac sign of Virgo, the Virgin.

The ancient model, that of Isis, is manifested in these words: *"I am the mother and the whole nature, the lady of all the elements, origin and beginning of all ages, supreme divinity, queen of the manes, first among the inhabitants of heaven, the unique type of gods or goddesses."*

(1) The Manes or manus, according to H.P. Blavatsky, are the personification of divine thought; each Manu is the special god, the creator, and shaper of everything that appears during their respective cycle of existence, or Manvantara. The Manes represent evolutionary, biological, and geomorphological cycles that humanity has been able to observe over millennia.

Isis was depicted wearing a headdress formed by two bovine horns with a disk in between. Her sacred animal was the cow, reminding us of her other rulership in the zodiac sign of Taurus.

According to Apuleius, her robes were woven with linen of extreme fineness and were dyed with all kinds of varied and mixed colors. As soon as they acquired the sparkling whiteness of the snow that covers the fields, like the yellow color of the ripe ears of the crops, associating with the time of the harvests, the time of harvest and collection of cereals, time of Virgo. On other occasions, her clothes were inflamed with a pinkish purple color of the fertile springtime lands colored by poppies – in clear reference to her other domain in Taurus.

This same archetype or divinity, was identified by the Greeks as Demeter, deus mater, mother goddess, and later as Cybele in Celtic mythology. In the myth, it is narrated that The God-father (Zeuspiter, Jupiter or Zeus) had a Mother Goddess (Deus mater) by his side (Demeter, Ceres or Cybele), from this common mother, the generating Earth, are born human beings, animals and plants. Demeter of the Greeks, Ceres of the Romans, or

Celtic Cybele tell us of the same model, of the same divinity and always refer to Mother Earth.

For the Greeks, Demeter was also a representation of the fertile and cultivated land, – fertile in Taurus and cultivated in Virgo–, she appeared as the goddess of fruits and the goods that agriculture provides. She was mainly the goddess of grains and fruits. She favored agricultural labor and the harvest.

In ancient representations, she appears with a dress that reaches to her feet, with a veil (the veil of Isis) that covers her head, while in other images she wears a crown of ears of corn or girdles her temples with a ribbon. Her attributes are the scepter, a sheaf of ears of corn, a torch, and the well-known veil.

The symbol of the scepter means power and authority; the torch is a symbol of purification, enlightenment, or transformation, and it is also a symbol of search and inquiry.

The ears of corn in the first interpretation represent the brightest star of the constellation of Virgo, Spica, the ear of corn, symbolizes the son who emerges from the earth, is a symbol of growth and fertility, both food and seed, it also symbolizes the natural cycle of death and rebirth.

The veil, which is the most particular symbol, speaks of hidden things, of secrets. It represents the temptation to unveil, to know, it is the incitement to knowledge. "A man managed to lift the veil of the goddess. But what did he see? He saw the miracle of miracles; himself". The removal of the veil or the successive veils of this divinity, represents the revelation of light. To be able to lift the veil means becoming immortal.

In Celtic mythology, Cybele was represented accompanied by two lions – as represented in the square of the same name in Madrid and another equal in Mexico City –. The two lions represent the second creative power of the second zodiac sign, Taurus.

The oldest sanctuary erected in her honor in Didyma was located inside a cave. Its relationship with the depths of the caves is repeated in the myth of Demeter and the cult of the pre-Christian black virgins. Therefore, as I said before, we assimilate all these models into one, whether they be Demeter, Cybele, Isis, or the Virgin of Montserrat, in all cases it is the same divinity of nature, considered as a woman, and for that reason, they also called her the "Goddess of infinite names". In the cave of Dindimo, as in the one of Montserrat, there was a primitive image carved in black stone "fallen from the sky", possibly from a meteorite.

In her legends, she is described as a woman with a beautiful face, with a touch of severity, whose hair, blonde as ripe ears of corn, could barely be dispelled.

Poseidon (Neptune) courted her, but the Pisces did not please her, however, the god of deception managed to metamorphose and join her. From this sporadic and repetitive union, the horse Arion (1) was born. Demeter took this matter as a serious offense that led her to Olympus and took refuge in the depths of the earth. It was the intervention of Zeus who forced her to return to the divine abode.

Zeus in turn also made her the object of his love and Demeter opposed the same resistance, but the lord of the gods managed to seduce her by metamorphosing into a bull.

Again this relationship or preference for the Bull or the zodiac sign of Taurus appears. From this union, Core the young woman was born, who later will be Persephone wife of Hades. Regent of the opposite sign, Scorpio.

(1) Arion was the mythical horse that was raised by the Nereids, Neptune gave it to the king of Aliaste and he gave it to Hercules. This horse had legs like a man and the use of speech.

In her legend, other romances are also told, she joined the hero Jason in the fields of fertile field, from which Pluto was born, a representation of wealth.

After the kidnapping of her daughter, she wandered in search of her, dressed in a black veil. In these pilgrimages, she arrived in Eleusis where the feasts in her honor with the Eleusinian mysteries were established.

The Eleusinian mysteries were associated with the cycle of the seasons, the growth of cereals, and vegetation in general. It was related to the mystery of life, death, and the afterlife.

These festive celebrations were held on two key dates; the lesser mysteries in spring (Taurus) as initiation rites, or the greater mysteries at the end of summer (Virgo). These two dramas centered around the kidnapping of Persephone who was taken to the underworld. "Her grieving mother, Demeter, went from here to there in her search, carrying a lit torch to illuminate the deep cracks in the earth, where she could have sunk. Her grief was so great that she stopped making the earth fruitful, to the point of causing universal hunger."

Disguised as an old woman, she finally arrived in Eleusis. There she met the daughters of King Keleos, who took her to their home, where she became the nanny of Demophon, the younger brother of those girls and the king's youngest son.

Demeter began the task of making Demophon immortal, secretly feeding him ambrosia, the food of the gods, during the day, and putting him in the fire at night to eliminate his mortality. This operation was interrupted by the mother, terrified to see her son in flames, and Demeter revealed her identity. Then she abandoned her intentions of making Demophon immortal, but before leaving the palace, she ordered the people of Eleusis to build a sanctuary on the hill, next to the "fountain of virginity", where she had met Keleos' daughters.

At that fountain, the rites that she taught her worshippers were to be celebrated, to achieve immortality for all who were initiated into those mysteries.

The main objective of those liturgical dramas was the renewal of vitality as a process of regeneration. In another sense, it was an agrarian festival centered on the goddess of fertility, who was at the same time the dispenser of immortality, but over time it became an esoteric mystery of death and resurrection.

Both in the myth of Demeter and the myth of Isis, the same characteristics appear; the incessant search of Isis for the remains of Osiris or Demeter for her daughter, in both cases clearly express a message of search, investigation, or inquiry that will imbue the people who are close to this divine model.

From these myths, the following character traits can be extracted for people of Virgo.

INQUISITIVE. – Of great curiosity, he feels inclined to investigate the origin and functioning of things.

REVERENT.– He feels great respect in his spirit towards authority, fame, and the position of others, or towards those qualities that he believes are worthy of admiration.

EXAMINING.- His investigative temperament leads him to scrutinize things and people to see if they have any defects or not.

REPAIRER.- He possesses great faculties for analyzing the parts of a whole and for being able to reassemble or repair things using that faculty.

DISPENSARY.- He is moved by the misfortune and real needs of others to whom he offers his help, always trying to be useful and putting his knowledge at the service of others.

SENSIBLE.- Prudent, and moderate, he has a view of reality without exaggerations or extremisms, which makes him the ideal conversationalist and advisor.

MEASURED.- He is not a friend of any waste, neither physical, nor psychic, nor economic. Measured in everything, his means are always proportional to the end he pursues.

DECENT.- He is respectful in his dealings and always has a touch of punctiliousness.

HUMBLE.- He lacks pride and vanity, rather he sins of an underestimation of his abilities and qualities that makes him stay in the background. This allows him to escape from burdens and responsibilities, which he could assume with perfect aptitude, and it enables him to appreciate the points of view and opinions of others.

COMPLAINER.- His strong critical and perfectionist spirit pushes him to always lament something past, present, or future about himself or others.

A Masculine Model For Libra Osiris-Dionysus

Libra and the asteroid belt

In my opinion, each zodiac sign has a pair of celestial bodies as rulers, one with feminine archetypal content and another masculine model.

The model of Venus-Urania is sufficiently known in the sign of Libra, but it is insufficient to understand the behavioral patterns of the men of this sign.

Our cultural modality associates planets with gods and these with archetypes or human models.

The masculine model that can be adapted to the zodiac sign of Libra is that of Osiris-Dionysus.

Osiris is one of the best-known Egyptian divinities, Plutarch tells us that when Osiris reigned, he brought the Egyptians out of their existence of deprivation and wild beasts, introduced them to the fruits of the earth, gave them laws teaching them to respect the gods. Later he traveled all over the earth to civilize it.

Osiris, which at first may seem to us to be a forgotten archetype, is none other than Dionysus, as Plutarch affirms. Dionysus is the god of vegetation, of the vine, of wine. "He is the one who spreads joy in abundance." Dionysus symbolizes the breaking of inhibitions, repressions, and rejections. Both in the myth of Osiris and in that of Dionysus, he travels all over the earth to civilize it and rarely had to resort to the force of arms, he generally used the force of persuasion, and reasoning, and was sometimes enchanted with his songs. For this reason, the

Greeks claimed that Osiris was the same god as Dionysus. Where else does the playful spirit that dwells in Libra natives come from?

-If we observe Libra people widely, we will see those civilizing characteristics, they tend to be people who rarely have to use force, they use persuasion, enchant others, and resort to reasoning and art.-

For the Egyptians, Osiris represents the principle and power of all that is moist, the cause of all generations, and the substance of all germ. They represented it using a scepter and an eye, the first emblem means power, power, and the second foresight. The hawk is also a representation of Osiris. This bird defeats all others for the liveliness of its gaze, the speed of its flight, and the little food it needs to live.

Osiris married his sister, Isis, although Plutarch says that Isis and Osiris, in love with each other, united before they were born in the womb of their mother.

Seth (the evil genius and brother of Osiris) who envied the throne to his brother, conspired against him, killed him, dismembered him, and ordered his dismembered corpse to be scattered.

(This dismemberment of a god is analogous to the destruction and fragmentation of the planet Phaeton, today the asteroid belt)

The myth tells that upon learning of this, Isis searched tirelessly until she found all the remains of her brother and husband except the phallus, which the evil genius had thrown into the river and had been devoured by three types of fish (those that the Egyptians do not eat) To replace the member, Isis made an imitation to conceive her son Horus. In this way, they consecrated the goddess Phallus and celebrated a feast in her honor. Statues of Osiris can be seen all over Egypt, represented in human form, with the erect virile member.

The cult of the phallus is repeated in Dionysian myths. Plutarch says, "Dionysus, as the sovereign and lord of the watery nature, is also called *'yea'* *'watery'*, being this god Osiris himself." He adds in his writing: "Clea, who can know better than you that Osiris is the same as Dionysus since you are the first among the Thyiads of Delphi and your father and mother consecrated to the Osiriac Mysteries?

If there is a need to provide evidence for others, let us leave the secret teachings in their place, and be content to affirm that what the priests openly do when they bury the bull Apis, when they transport its body on a raft, is no different from what happens at the festival of Bacchus. Indeed, they dress in fawnskins, carry thyrsus staffs, shout and behave like those possessed by Dionysus when they celebrate their orgies."

There is another tale that is narrated in Egypt. It is said that Apophis, the brother of the Sun, declared war on Zeus. Osiris came to Zeus' aid, helping him defeat his enemy. Then Zeus adopted Osiris as his son, calling him Dionysus. Additionally, the Greeks consecrate ivy to Dionysus; this plant is called *"chenosiris,"* which means *"Plant of Osiris"* in Egyptian.

In their sacred hymns in honor of Osiris, the Egyptians invoked "He who hides in the arms of the Sun." On the 30th day of the month of Epiph, when the Moon and the Sun are in the same straight line, they celebrate the festival called "The Birth of Horus." And on the 22nd day of the month of Faolf, after the autumn equinox, they celebrate the "Birth of the Sun's rays" (the entry of the Sun into Libra).

First and foremost, Dionysus was considered the god of vegetation and especially of life in trees. The Greeks considered him the god of ivy, the protector of trees and bushes, especially the vine. He was also the god of moisture and the liquid principle. His cult was associated with all rituals done in honor of the deities of springs, fountains, streams, torrents, and rivers.

Just like Osiris, Dionysus is a civilizing and playful god. He was called *Polites, Demosios, and Demoteles,* who presided over the organization of demos and cities. He played a preponderant role in the arts. Bacchic intoxication had a lot to do with musical and poetic inspiration. In Athens, he was the god of flute music, and the god of singing, he was also called the god of the choirs. All artists of singing, dancing, lyrical declamation, and poetry, were grouped under the name of Dionysian artists.

Dionysus was also called *Bacchus* in Rome, and Bacchus for us. He was the god of the vine because they say that one day this curious and cheerful god found a delicate plant on his way that he found sympathetic for its small, elongated stems. As it was a very small plant, it was only green shoots, to protect it and take it with him, he transplanted it inside a small nightingale bone. A few days later the plant grew and seeing that the pot had become too small for it, he transplanted it to a larger bone, this time he found a lion bone. A few weeks later the plant had grown so much that he had to transplant it to a bone of a much larger donkey femur. The adult plant gave its grape. Then the god, increasingly interested, discovered how to transform those grapes into wine, and the wonderful liquor was born with the qualities of the beings to whom their pots had corresponded; joy, strength, and stupidity.

That is why it was said that the one who drinks a little rejoices like a nightingale, the one who drinks a lot feels strong and bold like a lion and the one who drinks to excess becomes stupid like a donkey. It is also said that jackdaws were sacrificed in his honor because wine makes one speak indiscreetly.

-The last Libra man I have met is a Chilean astrologer who came to visit our country. Do you know what he gave me? !!A bottle of Chilean wine!!

During the country festivals in honor of Dionysus, the phallus, a symbol of productive force, was triumphantly paraded. In Athens, festivals in his honor were also celebrated with joyful and scandalous processions that sang loudly the *failkon* (song in honor of the phallus), very similar to the ones celebrated by the Egyptians in honor of Osiris.

In a similar fashion to Osiris, Dionysus was torn apart by the Titans (reminding us once again of his relationship with the planet that was torn apart and transformed into the asteroid belt). Zeus ordered Apollo to search for and gather his pieces, but just like in the myth of Osiris, the phallus was missing.

Several myths tell that his punishment consisted of provoking madness. One of the legends narrates that he gave a vine to King Ikarios, who planted it and made wine, and then he went out to share the precious liquid in the fields. However, the peasants drank excessively, and feeling its strange effects, they thought they were poisoned and killed Ikarios. Dionysus punished them by sending attacks of madness to young women, leading them to hang themselves. In another legend, he drives the daughters of King Minias crazy, and in yet another, the women of Argos go mad and tear apart their children.

This punishment, typical of Dionysus, is the weapon that Libras use against their enemies, partners, and sometimes even their friends. The maddening behavior of others is not exclusive to Libra males, but encompasses both sexes, like the rest of the symbolism.

Dionysus is the god of gentle and intoxicating induction. When not even Mars could defeat Hephaestus, Dionysus achieved what Mars couldn't through gentleness, diplomacy, and good wine.

It is in Libra where this inducing, inciting, provoking, or persuading ability fits the most, making others do what they probably wouldn't dare to do themselves.

But this model also gives Libra that playful touch that they retain until old age, that instinct for play, for jokes, for mischievous humor. That which gives them a childish and fun tone for others and makes them very pleasant to deal with.

They also receive from this archetype their malicious character and their propensity to not think well of the intentions of others and to distrust the reasons that make them approach them. In the same way as the two ancestral models, Libra have a wandering sprout, they like to wander and it is almost impossible for them to remain in one place or job for a long time. In general, they tend to be uprooted, they do not carry moorings, or emotions that attach them to people or things, on the contrary, their volatile intellect allows them little fidelity to places and beings.

They are seductive, they possess an irresistible attraction for their sympathy, intelligence, sense of timing, and witty expressiveness, but they are also disturbing and often disturb the order and harmony of things and tend to prevent or cut off the dialogue of the person who is speaking. They back down from situations that require a quick decision or a strenuous and persevering action. And finally, they have that special quality of inductors that makes them push others towards situations that attract them internally, but that they do not dare to confess or carry out on their own.